Inspection Lot Completion

201
Q&A

SAP Certified Application Associate
PLM-QM

ALSO BY BILLIE G. NORDMEYER

Inspection Lot Completion

201
Q&A

SAP Certified Application Associate
PLM-QM

Billie G. Nordmeyer, MBA, MA

Copyright © 2014 by Billie G. Nordmeyer

First Edition, 2014

Library of Congress Cataloging in Publication Data has been applied for.

ISBN 13: 978-1503137318
ISBN 10: 1503137317

Trademarks

Terms that are referred to in this book, which are known trademarks or service marks, are capitalized. The trademarks are the property of their owners. The inclusion in the book of any term that is a known trademark should not be thought to affect the validity of the trademark. The author of this book is not associated with any product or vendor mentioned in this book.

SAP EC is neither the author nor the publisher of this book, or affiliated with the author or publisher of this book in any way. Nor is SAP EC responsible for the content of the book. The book's content reflects the views of the author and not that of SAP EC. Any omissions or inaccuracies that might be present in this book, which do not correctly depict SAP EC or its products, are purely accidental, without maleficent intent.

Warning and Disclaimer

The author and publisher of this book have taken every precaution to ensure the content of the book is accurate and complete. Neither the author nor the publisher, however, assume any responsibility for inaccurate or inadequate information or for errors, inconsistencies or omissions in this book. Nor do the author or publisher assume any liability or responsibility to any person or entity for any damages or losses that result from the use of information published in this book. Neither the author nor the publisher guarantees that the use of the book will ensure that a candidate will pass any exam.

ABOUT THE AUTHOR

Billie G. Nordmeyer, MBA, MA is an SAP consultant, trainer and published author. She has held Senior Consultant and Business Development Manager of SAP Practice positions with a "Big 4" consulting firm, three "Fortune 100" firms and six "Fortune Most Admired Companies." Nordmeyer has consulted with Fortune 100 and Fortune 500 enterprises and supported clients in the aerospace, oil and gas, software, retail, pharmaceutical and manufacturing industries. Nordmeyer holds a BSBA in accounting, an MBA in finance and an MA in international management.

CONTENTS

INTRODUCTION

If your goal is a position with a consulting firm, a major firm in industry or a leading not-for-profit organization, an SAP certification will help you get there. Because many employers consider a technical certification a valuable employee achievement, certification exam training is available both online and at bricks-and-mortar institutions. But following your training, these resources leave it to you to identify a means to determine if you've grasped the essentials to the degree required to perform well during the testing process.

How important is it to confirm your understanding of concepts presented in training classes and by training documentation? In a certification exam setting, questions may bear little resemblance to the way major concepts are presented in the day-to-day operation of an SAP ECC module or solution. Consequently, while in your professional life you may play a key functional role in support of a module or solution and be proficient in spotting issues with an individual process on a daily basis, you'll need a global view of interrelated functions to do well on the exam.

As a certification candidate, you should also be aware that SAP certification exams assume you're knowledgeable about definitions and master data, as well as the application of a fairly extensive set of transactions and customizing functions. For example, during the testing process, you may be expected to recognize specific attributes of major transactions and customizing functions, definitions of key system elements, as well as the interrelationship among all of these factors.

What's more, when sitting for the certification exam and the answer to each question is one of several different -- and often complex -- alternatives, you want to be assured ahead of time that you can make the right choice. Reviewing documentation, however, does not provide you with the practical skills needed to apply your knowledge in a multiple-choice testing environment. In addition, the system-certification exam cram books that provide as few as 200 questions to test your knowledge of all of the relevant issues and all components that are focused on in one certification exam provide minimum help in this regard.

Hence this book series for the SAP Certified Application Consultant PLM-QM exam that allows you to test your knowledge using hundreds of multiple-choice questions well before you take the actual exam. The 201 Q&A SAP Certified Application Consultant PLM-QM book series is composed of individual books, each of which addresses one function or one type of master data that's covered in the certification exam. The advantage of this system over other training methods is the ability to focus only on the specific area where you need practice. Each study guide, such as Calibration Inspections and Quality Costs, provides 201 multiple choice questions, with both a short and detailed answer for each question. Each detailed answer states why the answer is correct, which allows you to grasp the bigger picture and use the knowledge you have gained through the testing process to increase your score on the actual exam.

I wish you the best of luck on the exam!

CHAPTER I

QUESTIONS

QUESTIONS

Q-1:   Which of the following is a function that is performed by the system as a usage decision for an inspection lot is recorded?

A. Record defects

B. Update PMIS

C. Calculate quality score for inspection lot

Short Answer: 94
Answer & Explanation: 113

Q-2:   Which of the following is a function that you can perform as you document a usage decision? Select all that apply.

A. Reverse stock posting

B. Activate quality notification

C. Record stock posting

D. Use worklist to record inspection results

E. Determine defective quantity for an inspection type

Short Answer: 94
Answer & Explanation: 113

Q-3:   The calculation of a quality score for an inspection lot and the update of inspection stages for a subsequent inspection lot are examples of what?

A. Automatic functions performed at the entry of defect records for the inspection lot

B. Automatic functions performed at the entry of a usage decision for the inspection lot

C. Automatic functions performed at the entry of inspection results for characteristics

Short Answer: 94
Answer & Explanation: 114

Q-4:   How are follow-up actions pertaining to quality-related defects defined?

A. Customizing application is used to link follow-up actions to usage decision codes

B. Change Group Code transaction is used to link follow-up actions to usage decision codes

C. Customizing application is used to create follow-up actions

D. Create Code Group transaction is used to create usage decision codes

Short Answer: 94
Answer & Explanation: 114

Q-5:   What function can be used to record the number of defective units in an inspection lot? Select all that apply.

A. Results Recording

B. Usage Decision

C. Defects Recording

Short Answer: 94
Answer & Explanation: 115

Q-6: How would you complete a quality inspection if the likely usage of a material is not known? Select all that apply.

A. Complete the inspection without a usage decision and with open characteristics

B. Complete the inspection without a usage decision and with closed characteristics

C. Complete short-term inspection

D. Discontinue inspection

Short Answer: 94
Answer & Explanation: 115

Q-7: The automatic proposal for a stock posting to unrestricted use stock should occur. How should this requirement be implemented? Select all that apply.

A. Stock proposal control indicator in catalog type 3 set code

B. Background processing control indicator in catalog type 3 set code

C. Change batch status control indicator in catalog type 3 set code

D. Background processing control indicator in catalog type 2 set code

E. Stock proposal control indicator in catalog type 5 set code

Short Answer: 94
Answer & Explanation: 116

Q-8:   The customer wants to complete more than one inspection lot simultaneously. What is required to accommodate this objective?

A. Multiple selection option for usage decision function

B. Evaluation function for inspection characteristics

C. Worklist function

Short Answer: 94
Answer & Explanation: 117

Q-9:   What is a requirement to create a proposal for an automatic stock posting?

A. Stock proposal control indicator in catalog type 3 set code

B. Background processing control indicator in catalog type 3 set code

C. Change batch status control indicator in catalog type 3 set code

D. Background processing control indicator in catalog type 2 set code

E. Stock proposal control indicator in catalog type 5 set code

Short Answer: 94
Answer & Explanation: 117

Q-10:   To track appraisal costs incurred at a work center for activities that are performed in an inspection operation, a QM order is created and assigned to which of the following?

A. Inspection Lot

B. Material

C. Work center

Short Answer: 94
Answer & Explanation: 118

Q-11:   At what point can you confirm values for inspection types to a QM order?

A. Defects recording

B. Results recording

C. Usage decision

Short Answer: 94
Answer & Explanation: 118

Q-12:   You want to enter the usage decision for an inspection lot. What must have occurred to enable you to do so? Select all that apply.

A. Release of inspection lot

B. Valuation of required inspection characteristics defined for inspection lot

C. Valuation of optional inspection characteristics defined for inspection lot

D. Status of inspection characteristics must permit entry of usage decision

E. User authorization to process required certificate

Short Answer: 95
Answer & Explanation: 119

Q-13: What statement is true regarding the entry of a usage decision for an inspection lot? Select all that apply.

A. A required certificate must be received prior to the entry of usage decision

B. Usage decision can be made irrespective of unvaluated inspection points

C. Inspection lot is released after entry of usage decision

D. Inspection lot status is changed after entry of usage decision to indicate release of inspection lot

Short Answer: 95
Answer & Explanation: 119

Q-14: In what sequence do the following activities related to a reversal of a stock posting occur?

A. Entry of usage decision for inspection lot

B. Cancellation of inspection lot

C. Stock posted from inspection stock to unrestricted use stock

D. Creation of return delivery with reference to original purchase order

A. ABCD

B. ACDB

C. BACD

Short Answer: 95
Answer & Explanation: 120

Q-15: You want to enter a usage decision for an inspection lot. How does the system determine if the entry should be allowed? Select all that apply. Select all that apply.

A. Inspection lot status is "Active"

B. Inspection lot status is "Released"

C. Required and optional inspection characteristics have been valuated

D. User is granted authorization for transaction

Short Answer: 95
Answer & Explanation: 121

Q-16: What transaction allows you to both valuate inspection points and enter a usage decision for an inspection lot?

A. Results Recording

B. Usage Decision

C. Defects Recording

Short Answer: 95
Answer & Explanation: 121

Q-17:   You want to enter a usage decision for an inspection lot. How would you deal with unvaluated inspection points?

A. Record usage decision

B. Discontinue inspection

C. Valuate outstanding inspection points and then record usage decision

D. Any of the above

E. None of the above

Short Answer: 95
Answer & Explanation: 122

Q-18:   The customer wants the ability to confirm that all quality notifications have been activated that should be activated for defects that were documented for an inspection lot. How will they do so?

A. Usage Decision function - Overview of Characteristics

B. Usage Decision function - Overview of Defects

C. Usage Decision function - Display Related Notifications

Short Answer: 95
Answer & Explanation: 123

Q-19: In what case can a usage decision for an inspection lot be entered?

A. Status of inspection lot is "active"

B. User authorization to enter usage decision

C. Goods receipt is confirmed

Short Answer: 95
Answer & Explanation: 123

Q-20: How does the customer confirm that all the quality notifications have been activated that should have been activated for critical defects identified during a quality inspection?

A. Results Recording function - Display Related Notifications

B. Defects Recording function - Display Related Notifications

C. Usage Decision function - Display Related Notifications

Short Answer: 95
Answer & Explanation: 124

Q-21: A defect record that is recorded during a calibration inspection can be activated as a_____?

A. Quality notification

B. Service notification

C. Maintenance notification

Short Answer: 95
Answer & Explanation: 125

Q-22:   The creation of a follow-up action to address a documented defect triggers which of the following?

A. Update to inspection lot status to reflect the status of follow-up action

B. Update to inspection characteristic status to reflect status of follow-up action

C. Update to inspection operation status to reflect status of follow-up action

Short Answer: 95
Answer & Explanation: 125

Q-23:   A customer wants to view the characteristic inspection results for multiple inspection lots that have been processed. What is required to do so?

A. Select the Characteristics tab in the Usage Decision menu

B. Select the Evaluations tab in the Logistics QM Information System menu

C. Select the Characteristics tab in the Results Recording menu

D. Select the Characteristics tab in the Inspection Results menu

Q-24:   The customer wants to view the stock in an inspection lot and then post the inspected materials to the appropriate stock account. How will he do so?

A. Usage Decision function - Overview of Stocks

B. Defects Recording function - Overview of Stocks

C. Results Recording function - Overview of Stocks

Q-25:   An inspection point may refer to which of the following? Select all that apply.

A. Stability sample

B. Equipment

C. Functional location

D. Inspection quantity

Q-26:   Which of the following is an option that can be executed if the inspection lot contains unvaluated inspection points? Select all that apply.

A. Enter usage decision

B. Discontinue inspection

C. Valuate inspection points and enter usage decision

D. Complete inspection lot on short-term basis

Short Answer: 96
Answer & Explanation: 127

Q-27:   The customer wants a list of any stock that was assigned to a stock-relevant inspection lot. How can you accommodate this requirement?

A. Usage Decision - Overview of Stocks

B. Results Recording - Material Documents

C. Evaluations - Extras for Material Documents

Short Answer: 96
Answer & Explanation: 128

Q-28:   The quantity of material in an inspection lot, the quantity of material posted with a usage decision, and the quantity of material transferred from storage location A to storage location B is documented how?

A. Inspection lot

B. Material master record

C. Inspection characteristic

D. Material document

Short Answer: 96
Answer & Explanation: 128

Q-29:   Which of the following is an Inspection Lot Completion component function that is used to first display stock that has been posted to or from a particular inspection lot and then post additional stock?

A. Results Recording

B. Defects Recording

C. Usage Decision

Short Answer: 96
Answer & Explanation: 129

Q-30:   What step in the inspection process can be used to display inspection characteristic results for all characteristics in a task list?

A. Usage Decision

B. Results Recording

C. Defects Recording

Short Answer: 96
Answer & Explanation: 129

Q-31:   What step in the inspection process can be used to view the stock in an inspection lot as well as enter stock postings for the selected material?

A. Defects Recording

B. Results Recording

C. Usage Decision

Short Answer: 96
Answer & Explanation: 130

Q-32:   A customer wants a list of material documents created as stock was posted when an inspection lot was created. What list provides this information?

A. Results Recording – Material Documents

B. Usage Decision – Material Documents

C. Evaluations – Material Documents

Short Answer: 96
Answer & Explanation: 130

Q-33:   The customer discovers that an error was made during a goods receipt posting. As a result of this error, the stock posting to blocked stock for an inspection lot is incorrect. Which of the following activities must now occur to correct this error? Select all that apply.

A. Create transfer posting from blocked stock to unrestricted use stock in Quality Management

B. Cancel inspection lot in Quality Management

C. Create return delivery for purchase order in Inventory Management

D. Create goods receipt posting in Inventory Management

Short Answer: 96
Answer & Explanation: 131

Q-34:   Why is the Overview of Defects used with the Usage Decision function? Select all that apply.

A. Create list of defect records created for inspection lot

B. Identify defect types documented in defect records for an inspection lot

C. Activate notifications on the basis of the defect class of the defect code

D. Activate Quality Notifications on the basis of the defect class of the defect type

Short Answer: 96
Answer & Explanation: 132

Q-35: Which of the following is used to automatically enter a usage decision for an inspection lot?

A. Program executed with job management function

B. Customizing setting

C. Usage Decision transaction

Short Answer: 96
Answer & Explanation: 132

Q-36: A customer tracks stock using serial numbers. How does the system address the stock posting to unrestricted use stock from inspection stock for three units of material, each of which has an assigned serial number?

A. Each individual unit must be posted to unrestricted use stock and four object lists are assigned to the individual material documents

B. The four units can be posted to unrestricted use stock as a group and one object list can be assigned to the individual material document(s)

C. Each individual unit must be posted to unrestricted use stock and one object list is assigned to individual material document(s)

D. The four units can be posted to unrestricted use stock as a group
and four object lists are assigned to individual material document(s)

Short Answer: 96
Answer & Explanation: 133

Q-37:   What is a requirement to complete an inspection automatically? Select all that apply.

A. No inspection lot characteristic was rejected in the inspection lot

B. All characteristics were confirmed and closed or closed on a short-term basis

C. Defect records were created for critical defects and activated as notifications during the inspection

Short Answer: 96
Answer & Explanation: 133

Q-38:   A quality score can be calculated on what basis?

A. Quality score for inspection characteristics

B. Usage decision code

C. Share of defects for inspection type

Short Answer: 97
Answer & Explanation: 134

Q-39:   Some, but not all inspection points have been valuated. What processing options does the user have at this point? Select all that apply.

A. Enter the usage decision for the inspection lot

B. Enter the usage decision for the valuated inspection points

C. Delete the inspection lot and create new lot referencing the valuated inspection points

Short Answer: 97
Answer & Explanation: 135

Q-40:   A worklist function can be used in relation to which of the following?

A. Enter stock posting prior to the entry of a usage decision for an inspection lot

B. Enter stock posting simultaneously with the entry of a usage decision for an inspection lot

C. Enter stock posting after the entry of a usage decision for an inspection lot

Short Answer: 97
Answer & Explanation: 135

Q-41:   In what circumstance is stock posted to sample usage?

A. Material is assigned to an inspection lot

B. Material is destroyed in an inspection

C. Material is assigned to a sample reserve

D. Material is a "New Material"

Short Answer: 97
Answer & Explanation: 136

Q-42:   Which of the following can be specified as the destination for quantities of material from an inspection lot? Select all that apply.

A. Sample usage

B. Return delivery

C. Unblocked stock

D. Restricted use stock

Short Answer: 97
Answer & Explanation: 136

Q-43:   How does the system determine the account to which the stock in an inspection lot should be posted? Select all that apply.

A. Control indicator in characteristic

B. Control indicator in usage decision code

C. Control indicator in material master record

D. Control indicator in material document

Short Answer: 97
Answer & Explanation: 137

Q-44: How does the system determine if a stock posting to unrestricted use stock should occur automatically?

A. Control indicator in characteristic

B. Control indicator in usage decision code

C. Control indicator in material master record

D. Control indicator in material document

Short Answer: 97
Answer & Explanation: 138

Q-45: What transaction determines the quantity of materials that was destroyed during an inspection, which is needed to make a stock posting?

A. Defects Recording

B. Results Recording

C. Usage Decision

Short Answer: 97
Answer & Explanation: 138

Q-46: Inspection stock was successfully posted to unrestricted material stock and material documents were created. However, the batch cannot be selected for shipment to a customer. Why?

A. The stock proposal indicator was not set in the catalog type 3 set code

B. The "background processing" control indicator was not set in the catalog type 3 set code

C. The "no change to batch status" control indicator was set in the class characteristic

D. The "no change to batch status" control indicator was set in the set code

E. The "no change to batch status" control indicator was set in the inspection lot header

Short Answer: 97
Answer & Explanation: 139

Q-47:   What function is integrated with the stock posting procedure? Select all that apply.

A. Defects Recording

B. Results Recording

C. Usage Decision

Short Answer: 97
Answer & Explanation: 139

Q-48:   What would you use to automatically determine the stock account to which material in an inspection lot is posted?

A. Stock proposal control indicator in the material master record inspection settings

B. Stock proposal control indicator in the inspection plan characteristic

C. Stock proposal control indicator in the material type

D. Stock proposal control indicator in the usage decision code

Short Answer: 97
Answer & Explanation: 140

Q-49:   You have decided that materials that are destroyed during a quality inspection should be posted to the sample usage account. Where is the control set that leads to this posting?

A. Catalog type 3 code

B. Characteristic

C. Inspection lot

D. Material master record

Short Answer: 97
Answer & Explanation: 140

Q-50:   The automatic posting of material to the sample usage stock account did not occur following the material inspection. What should be checked? Select all that apply.

A. Destructive inspection control indicator in the inspection characteristic

B. Stock proposal control indicator in the usage decision set code

C. Background processing control indicator in the usage decision set code

D. Batch status control indicator in the inspection characteristic

Short Answer: 97
Answer & Explanation: 141

Q-51:   What option can be used to ensure the batch status reflects the usage decision for the related inspection lot?

A. Batch status control indicator in the master inspection characteristic

B. Batch status control indicator in the catalog type 3 code

C. Batch status control indicator in the inspection lot header

D. Batch status control indicator in the material master record

Short Answer: 97
Answer & Explanation: 141

Q-52:   The customer wants to view a list of material documents that were created as an inspection lot was processed. What function is used to do so?

A. Results Recording

B. Usage Decision

C. Display Inspection Lot

Short Answer: 97
Answer & Explanation: 142

Q-53:   What statement is true regarding the list of material documents created for a stock-relevant inspection lot? Select all that apply.

A. The documents in the list account for the original stock posting for the creation of a stock-relevant inspection lot

B. The documents in the list account for a decrease to the original stock in an inspection lot

C. The documents in the list account for any stock transfer between work stations

Short Answer: 98
Answer & Explanation: 143

Q-54:   A material document is created with reference to what?

A. Inspection lot

B. Inspection operation

C. Inspection characteristic

Short Answer: 98
Answer & Explanation: 144

Q-55:   What function is used to access material documents that are created for a stock-relevant inspection lot?

A. Defects Recording

B. Results Recording

C. Usage Decision

Short Answer: 98
Answer & Explanation: 144

Q-56: In what case is the Usage Decision transaction used? Select all that apply.

A. Display Material Documents for Inspection Lots

B. Record Defective Quantity

C. Display Results for Inspection Lots

D. Reverse Stock Posting

Short Answer: 98
Answer & Explanation: 145

Q-57: What is the purpose of the sample usage stock account?

A. Stock account for stock blocked in quality inspection

B. Stock account for stock destroyed in quality inspection

C. Stock account for stock reserved for quality inspection

Short Answer: 98
Answer & Explanation: 145

Q-58: The system should post stock to the sample usage stock account for materials that were destroyed during a quality inspection. How is this requirement implemented? Select all that apply.

A. Destructive inspection for inspection characteristic control indicator

B. Stock proposal control indicator for usage decision set code

C. Background processing control indicator for usage decision code

D. Change batch status control indicator for usage decision set code

Short Answer: 98
Answer & Explanation: 146

Q-59: When a usage decision for an inspection lot is documented, how is it determined that a stock posting to unrestricted stock should occur automatically? Select all that apply.

A. Stock proposal indicator for usage decision code

B. Background processing indicator for usage decision code

C. Batch state indicator for usage decision code

Short Answer: 98
Answer & Explanation: 147

Q-60: A stock posting to unrestricted use stock should occur in the background at the valuation of an inspection lot. What procedures are required to perform this activity? Select all that apply.

A. Destructive inspection for inspection characteristic control indicator

B. Stock proposal control indicator for usage decision set code

C. Background processing control indicator for usage decision code

D. Change batch status control indicator for usage decision set code

Short Answer: 98
Answer & Explanation: 148

Q-61: Which statement is correct regarding an automatic proposal for a stock posting? Select all that apply.

A. Destructive inspection control indicator for inspection characteristic control indicator

B. Stock proposal control indicator for usage decision set code

C. Background processing control indicator for usage decision code

D. Batch status change control indicator for usage decision set code

Short Answer: 98
Answer & Explanation: 149

Q-62: Which of the following functions can be used to create a material document to document a stock posting?

A. Usage Decision

B. Results Recording

C. Defects Recording

Short Answer: 98
Answer & Explanation: 150

Q-63: Which of the following determines if a stock posting is processed in the background or if it is processed with a manual procedure? Select all that apply.

A. Stock posting proposal control indicator in usage decision set code

B. Batch status control indicator in usage decision set code

C. Background processing control indicator in usage decision set code

Short Answer: 99
Answer & Explanation: 150

Q-64: What is the purpose of the stock posting proposal control indicator in the Catalog Type 3 code?

A. Post stock to unrestricted use stock

B. Post stock to scrap

C. Post stock to blocked stock

D. Any of the above

E. None of the above

Short Answer: 99
Answer & Explanation: 151

Q-65: What criteria influences the entry of a usage decision for an inspection lot? Select all that apply.

39

A. Release of the inspection lot

B. Authorization of the user to enter the usage decision for the lot

C. Receipt of any optional certificate

Short Answer: 99
Answer & Explanation: 151

Q-66:   Which of the following is a consideration in a stock posting based on a usage decision for an inspection lot? Select all that apply.

A. Stock posting before, during or after usage decision

B. Stock posting for stock relevant material versus non-stock relevant material

C. Stock account to which material should be posted from an inspection lot

Short Answer: 99
Answer & Explanation: 152

Q-67:   What function in the inspection process can be used to display the defects that were confirmed for goods in an inspection lot as well as the related defect structure?

A. Defects Recording

B. Usage Decision

C. Results Recording

Short Answer: 99
Answer & Explanation: 152

Q-68:   You want to view defect records for an inspection lot. How do you do so?

A. Usage Decision: Overview of Defects

B. Results Recording: Overview of Defects

C. Defect Quality in Inspection Lot List

Short Answer: 99
Answer & Explanation: 153

Q-69:   Which of the following is a true statement(s) regarding the completion of an inspection with no usage decision? Select all that apply.

A. Inspection results can be changed for an inspection lot unless the inspection is completed without a usage decision

B. Inspection results can be entered for the inspection lot after it is completed on a short-term basis

C. All characteristics must be completed prior to the completion of the inspection without a usage decision

Short Answer: 99
Answer & Explanation: 154

Q-70:   When a stock posting is created, what data is entered in the material document?

A. Sample usage

B. Date of stock posting

C. Date of inspection lot

Short Answer: 99
Answer & Explanation: 155

Q-71: The customer wants to complete an inspection without entering a usage decision for the material in the lot. What function will enable them to do so?

A. Results Recording

B. Usage Decision

C. Reset Status

Short Answer: 99
Answer & Explanation: 155

Q-72: What criteria influences the reversal of a stock posting for an inspection lot?

A. Material in inspection lot was posted to blocked stock

B. Material in inspection lot was posted to restricted stock

C. Material in inspection lot was posted to sample usage

Short Answer: 99
Answer & Explanation: 156

Q-73: You want to enter a posting to new material stock for an inspection lot that is not stock relevant. What function can be used to do so?

A. Results Recording

B. Inspection Lot Completion

C. Usage Decision

D. All of the above

E. None of the above

Short Answer: 99
Answer & Explanation: 157

Q-74: What initial criteria must be entered to document a usage decision?

A. Inspection lot category

B. Inspection lot number

C. Inspection type

Short Answer: 99
Answer & Explanation: 157

Q-75: What function can be used to display the defect structure for an inspection lot?

A. Create Usage Decision

B. Change Usage Decision

C. Display Usage Decision

D. All of the above

E. None of the above

Short Answer: 99
Answer & Explanation: 158

Q-76: Which of the following is a valid function of the Inspection Lot Completion component? Select all that apply.

A. Overview of Inspection Operations

B. Complete Inspection on Short-term Basis

C. Change Inspection Results with History

D. Create Usage Decision

Short Answer: 100
Answer & Explanation: 159

Q-77: Which of the following is a valid function of the QM Inspection Lot Completion component?

A. Reverse Stock Posting

B. Reverse Material Document

C. Reverse Defect Record

Short Answer: 100
Answer & Explanation: 159

Q-78: What activity can be performed with the Usage Decision function? Select all that apply.

A. Confirm the receipt of a certificate

B. Create a quality notification

C. Display defect structure

D. Display characteristic results

E. Calculate quality score

Short Answer: 100
Answer & Explanation: 160

Q-79: The Overview of Defects is accessed by means of the Usage Decision function. What customer requirement is met by doing so? Select all that apply.

A. Determine the types of defects confirmed for an inspection lot

B. Determine the quality notifications that have been activated for an inspection lot

C. Determine the hierarchical level at which defect records were created

Short Answer: 100
Answer & Explanation: 161

Q-80: A quality score for an inspection lot is automatically calculated on what basis?

A. Usage decision code for the characteristic

B. Share of defects in inspection lot

C. Share of defects for characteristics

D. Quality score for operation

Short Answer: 100
Answer & Explanation: 162

Q-81: The inspection stages for an inspection lot are calculated on the basis of what?

A. Recorded defects

B. Inspection characteristic results

C. Quality level

D. Usage decision for the inspection lot

Short Answer: 100
Answer & Explanation: 162

Q-82: What function can be automatically performed when a usage decision for an inspection lot is made?

A. Calculate quality score for the inspection lot

B. Activate notification

C. Trigger follow-up actions

D. Update quality level

E. Enter stock posting

Short Answer: 100
Answer & Explanation: 163

Q-83: The use of the Inspection Lot Completion component requires the implementation of what other components? Select all that apply.

A. Batches

B. Production Planning

C. Catalogs

D. Controlling

E. Inspection Lot Creation

Short Answer: 100
Answer & Explanation: 164

Q-84:   You want to identify the characteristics or operations for which defects were confirmed. How would you do so?

A. Usage Decision - Defect Structure

B. Results Recording - Defect Structure

C. Defects Recording - Defect Structure

Short Answer: 100
Answer & Explanation: 164

Q-85:   A follow-up function can be triggered by what?

A. Usage decision code

B. Characteristic results

C. Defect confirmation

Short Answer: 100
Answer & Explanation: 165

Q-86:   What function allows the generation of a hierarchical tree structure that references both the defects and the defects recording levels for which defects were confirmed?

A. Overview of characteristics

B. Display defect structure

C. Activate quality notification

Short Answer: 100
Answer & Explanation: 166

Q-87:   What transaction directly leads to the update of a quality level record that in turn impacts the vendor evaluation?

A. Defects Recording

B. Results Recording

C. Usage Decision

Short Answer: 100
Answer & Explanation: 167

Q-88:   The calculation of a quality score for an inspection lot is determined by what?

A. Inspection type

B. Master inspection characteristic

C. Inspection operation

Short Answer: 100
Answer & Explanation: 167

Q-89:   What function can be used to access a Results History for a characteristic?

A. Defects Recording

B. Results Recording

C. Usage Decision

Short Answer: 100
Answer & Explanation: 168

Q-90: Which of the following is an activity that can be performed prior to the entry of the usage decision? Select all that apply.

A. Activate quality notification

B. Follow-up action

C. Calculate quality score

D. Create stock posting

E. Confirm activities for inspection operation

Short Answer: 101
Answer & Explanation: 169

Q-91: You want to simultaneously view any defect that was recorded for a particular inspection lot. What function would you use to do so?

A. Defects Recording

B. Results Recording

C. Usage Decision

Short Answer: 101
Answer & Explanation: 169

Q-92: In what case is the Usage Decision function used?

A. Create defect record

B. Update inspection lot status for inspection completion

C. Confirm activities for inspection operation

D. Enter quality score for characteristic

Short Answer: 101
Answer & Explanation: 170

Q-93: What is a restriction regarding a change to recorded inspection results? Select all that apply.

A. Recorded results cannot be changed subsequent to documentation of usage decision

B. Recorded results cannot be changed subsequent to inspection completion

C. Recorded results cannot be changed subsequent to short-term inspection completion

Short Answer: 101
Answer & Explanation: 171

Q-94: The acceptance or rejection of goods in an inspection lot is based on what?

A. Recorded results for required inspection characteristics

B. Recorded results for inspection lot

C. Recorded results for inspection type

Short Answer: 101
Answer & Explanation: 171

Q-95: What is a prerequisite to the completion of an inspection with a usage decision?

A. Release of inspection characteristics

B. Results recorded for required inspection characteristics

C. Authorization to record usage decision

D. Active status of inspection lot

Short Answer: 101
Answer & Explanation: 172

Q-96: A quality score formula is defined on what basis?

A. Material type

B. Inspection type

C. Stock type

Short Answer: 101
Answer & Explanation: 172

Q-97: What are examples of criteria that are used to determine if a characteristic is accepted or rejected?

A. Sample size

B. Acceptance number

C. Inspection type

Short Answer: 101
Answer & Explanation: 173

Q-98: When entering data for a usage decision, the overview of characteristics indicates that results have not been recorded for some required characteristics. What is the result?

A. Required characteristics must be closed prior to entry of the usage decision

B. Inspection lot status must be changed to allow entry of usage decision

C. Inspection lot status must be changed to long-term inspection completed

Short Answer: 101
Answer & Explanation: 173

Q-99: For what purpose is the Inspection Lot Completion component "Overview of Stocks for Inspection Lot" used?

A. Create stock posting

B. Display stock posting

C. Change stock posting

Short Answer: 101
Answer & Explanation: 174

Q-100: What usage decision report provides the ability to make a stock posting for a material in an inspection lot?

A. Overview of Characteristics

B. Overview of Inspection Points

C. Overview of Defects

D. Overview of Stocks

Short Answer: 101
Answer & Explanation: 174

Q-101:   The customer wants to view both the status of characteristics in an inspection lot and the valuation of the characteristics. What function will allow him to do so?

A. Usage Decision - Overview of Characteristics

B. Defects Recording - Overview of Characteristics

C. Results Recording - Overview of Characteristics

Short Answer: 101
Answer & Explanation: 175

Q-102:   What overview is accessed by means of the Usage Decision transaction? Select all that apply.

A. Overview of Characteristics

B. Overview of Defects

D. Overview of Stocks

E. Overview of Materials

E. Overview of Operations

Short Answer: 101
Answer & Explanation: 176

Q-103: T/F Defects can be recorded and a quality notification can be activated before or after the entry of a usage decision.

A. True

B. False

Short Answer: 101
Answer & Explanation: 177

Q-104: The customer wants to both view the defects that were recorded for a particular inspection characteristic and activate any quality notifications that may be required. What function will allow him to do so?

A. Defects Recording - Overview of Defects

B. Results Recording - Overview of Defects

C. Usage Decision - Overview of Defects

Short Answer: 102
Answer & Explanation: 177

Q-105: Identify an information screen that is related to an inspection lot, which can be accessed by means of the Usage Decision function.

A. Overview of Inspection Lot

B. Overview of Stocks

C. Overview of Defects

D. Overview of Operations

Short Answer: 102
Answer & Explanation: 178

Q-106: How would you determine the types of defects that have been recorded for an inspection lot?

A. Usage Decision - Overview of Defects

B. Defects Recording - Overview of Defects

C. Results Recording - Overview of Defects

Short Answer: 102
Answer & Explanation: 179

Q-107: What function can be used to review the types of defects that were confirmed for materials in an inspection lot?

A. Defects Recording

B. Usage Decision

C. Results Recording

Short Answer: 102
Answer & Explanation: 180

Q-108: The Overview of Stocks for Inspection Lot is used. What customer requirement is met by doing so?

A. Identify the types of defects that were confirmed for goods in the inspection lot

B. Identify the status of an inspection characteristic for the inspection lot

C. Identify the valuation of the characteristics for the inspection lot

D. Post a quantity of material to a particular stock type

Short Answer: 102
Answer & Explanation: 181

Q-109: The customer wants to document the results of an inspection that was originally completed as a short-term inspection. What is a prerequisite to the implementation of this requirement? Select all that apply.

A. Reset status of the inspection lot

B. Reset status of the inspection characteristic

C. Reset status of the inspection operation

Short Answer: 102
Answer & Explanation: 181

Q-110: An inspection lot includes inspection points that have not been valuated. What processing option does an authorized person have at this point? Select all that apply.

A. Valuate the inspection points and then make the usage decision

B. Make the usage decision

C. Discontinue the inspection

D. Complete inspection

E. Complete short-term inspection

Short Answer: 102
Answer & Explanation: 182

Q-111:   Which of the following is a requirement to enter a usage decision for an inspection lot that includes outstanding inspection points?

A. Valuation of inspection points

B. Discontinue the inspection

C. Authorization to make usage decision

Short Answer: 102
Answer & Explanation: 183

Q-112:   What must occur prior to the entry of the usage decision for an inspection lot?

A. Defects have been recorded

B. Quality notifications have been activated

C. Results have been recorded for required characteristics

Short Answer: 102
Answer & Explanation: 183

Q-113:   What is a prerequisite to the entry of a usage decision for an inspection lot? Select all that apply.

A. Confirmation of the receipt of a quality certificate

B. Recorded results for optional inspection characteristics

C. Release of inspection lot

D. User authorization for the transaction

Short Answer: 102
Answer & Explanation: 184

Q-114: Under what circumstances is it possible for you to enter a usage decision for an inspection lot? Select all that apply.

A. Status of the inspection lot is "Released"

B. Inspection results are recorded for required and optional inspection characteristics

C. Authorization to enter the usage decision

Short Answer: 102
Answer & Explanation: 184

Q-115: What statement regarding the entry of a usage decision for an inspection lot is correct? Select all that apply.

A. The same transaction can be used to both enter the usage decision and create a quality notification

B. It is not necessary to record all inspection results for required inspection characteristics for the inspection lot prior to the entry of the usage decision

C. The inspection lot must not be released prior to the entry of the usage decision

Short Answer: 102
Answer & Explanation: 185

Q-116: A customer requests a means to view not only the defects that were recorded during the inspection of a material but also the recording level at which the defects were documented. What function would make this data available to the customer?

A. Usage Decision - Overview of Defects

B. Usage Decision - Short-term Inspection

C. Usage Decision - Complete Inspection

Short Answer: 102
Answer & Explanation: 186

Q-117: Which of the following are included in the display of a defect structure?

A. The defects recorded for a characteristic

B. The defects recorded for an inspection lot

C. The defects recorded for an operation

Short Answer: 102
Answer & Explanation: 186

Q-118: How can the customer differentiate the defects that were recorded at the operation defect recording level versus those that were recorded at the characteristic level for a particular inspection lot?

A. Usage Decision - Overview of Defects

B. Defects Recording - Overview of Defects

C. Results Recording - Overview of Defects

Short Answer: 103
Answer & Explanation: 187

Q-119: What function would you use to activate an inactive quality notification that was created during a quality inspection?

A. Defects Recording

B. Results Recording

C. Usage Decision

Short Answer: 103
Answer & Explanation: 188

Q-120: What is the purpose of the activation of a quality notification?

A. Create defect record

B. Close defect record

C. Initiate corrective action

Short Answer: 103
Answer & Explanation: 189

Q-121: What step in the inspection process leads to the automatic entry of the valuation code and quality score for the inspection lot?

A. Creation of defect record

B. Entry of usage decision code

C. Entry of inspection results

Short Answer: 103
Answer & Explanation: 189

Q-122: What is the effect of the entry of the usage decision for an inspection lot?

A. Quality score is calculated

B. Follow-up action is copied into inspection lot

C. Inspection lot status is updated

D. Subsequent entries to record inspection results can be made

Short Answer: 103
Answer & Explanation: 190

Q-123: An automatic proposal for a stock posting is dependent on what settings? Select all that apply.

A. Batch status control indicator for the usage decision code

B. Background processing control indicator for the usage decision code

C. Stock proposal control indicator for the usage decision code

Short Answer: 103
Answer & Explanation: 191

Q-124: What would you use to display the inspection results for a single inspection lot?

A. Overview of Inspection Operations

B. Overview of Characteristics

C. Overview of Inspection Lot

Short Answer: 103
Answer & Explanation: 192

Q-125:   Which of the following is an option you can elect to execute with the usage decision transaction?

A.   Update quality level

B.   Activate quality notification

C.   Calculate quality score

Short Answer: 103
Answer & Explanation: 192

Q-126:   A customer wants a report that isolates the characteristics that are relevant to the usage decision for an inspection lot versus all characteristics defined for the lot. What function can be used for this purpose?

A.   Overview of Inspection Operations

B.   Overview of Characteristics

C.   Overview of Inspection Lot

Short Answer: 103
Answer & Explanation: 193

Q-127:   What is the purpose of the Inspection Lot Completion component function Overview of Characteristics? Select all that apply.

A. Provides the fields and functions necessary to make stock postings for the characteristics

B. Displays the inspection results for individual inspection characteristics in the inspection lot

C. Displays the valuation of the individual inspection characteristics in the inspection lot

Short Answer: 103
Answer & Explanation: 193

Q-128:   The customer selects the results history option in the Usage Decision transaction. What requirement is met by doing so? Select all that apply.

A. Display characteristics that pertain to the usage decision for the inspection lot

B. Display inspection results for a characteristic in chronological order

C. Display all characteristics in the task list

Short Answer: 103
Answer & Explanation: 194

Q-129:   A material document must be created for a stock posting. What user entries are necessary to create the document?

A. Purpose of stock posting

B. Date of stock posting

C. Date of material document

D. All of the above

E. None of the above

Short Answer: 103
Answer & Explanation: 194

Q-130: Which of the following leads to the creation of a material document when stock is posted before the usage decision is recorded? Select all that apply.

A. Stock posting to restricted-use stock

B. Stock posting to scrap

C. Stock posting to blocked stock

D. Stock posting to unblocked stock

Short Answer: 103
Answer & Explanation: 195

Q-131: Which of the following is a characteristic of a stock posting with the Usage Decision transaction? Select all that apply.

A. A manual or automatic process is used to make the stock posting

B. Postings in the Material Management component are made on the basis of stock postings entered in QM

C. Stock postings must occur before the usage decision

D. A material document must include a cost center

Short Answer: 103
Answer & Explanation: 196

Q-132: Which of the following is an example of an inspection lot that is not stock-relevant? Select all that apply.

A. Goods receipt blocked stock

B. Inspection lot that is created with a manual process

C. Delivery to customer

Short Answer: 104
Answer & Explanation: 196

Q-133: How do you display a chronological list of characteristic results?

A. Overview of Characteristics

B. Usage Decision Results History

C. Overview of Inspection Lot

Short Answer: 104
Answer & Explanation: 197

Q-134: A material document is created on what basis?

A. Inspection lot quantity correction

B. Stock transfer

C. Stock posting made with Defects Recording

Short Answer: 104
Answer & Explanation: 197

Q-135: What is a prerequisite for an automatic proposal for a stock posting associated with a usage decision?

A. Stock proposal control indicator for usage decision code

B. Background processing control indicator for usage decision code

C. Batch status change control indicator for usage decision code

Short Answer: 104
Answer & Explanation: 198

Q-136: The automatic proposal for a stock posting for a quantity of a material that is destroyed during an inspection can be triggered by what?

A. Results recording set code

B. Defect set code

C. Usage decision set code

Short Answer: 104
Answer & Explanation: 199

Q-137: What document is created as the result of a stock posting that is triggered when the inspection lot is created?

A. Goods receipt document

B. Material document

C. Stock transfer order

Short Answer: 104
Answer & Explanation: 199

Q-138: What must be specified to post stock for a single lot after a usage decision is entered?

A. Inspection lot number

B. Material number

C. Quantity of stock to be posted

Short Answer: 104
Answer & Explanation: 200

Q-139: What is the difference between posting stock before, during or after the usage decision is entered to the system? Select all that apply.

A. Ability to post stock for one inspection lot versus multiple inspection lots

B. Manual entry of stock posting versus use of worklist to post stocks

C. Increase in quantity posted versus decrease in quantity posted for desired stock types

Short Answer: 104
Answer & Explanation: 201

Q-140: Which of the following is a batch management function that pertains to the usage decision transaction?

A. Batch display

B. Batch where-used list

C. Post batch to new material

Short Answer: 104
Answer & Explanation: 201

Q-141: Which of the following is a requirement that enables the creation of a stock posting to unrestricted use stock from inspection stock for a serialized material? Select all that apply.

A. Creation of a serial number profile for movement type

B. Selection of single-unit inspection using serial numbers control indicator for material master inspection type

C. Assignment of serial number profile to material type

Short Answer: 104
Answer & Explanation: 202

Q-142:   Single units of material with a serial number can be selected and posted to which of the following stock accounts? Select all that apply.

A. Return delivery

B. New material

C. Scrap

D. All of the above

E. None of the above

Short Answer: 104
Answer & Explanation: 203

Q-143:   Where is the quality score stored? Select all that apply.

A. Material type

B. Material master record inspection type

C. Inspection lot record

Short Answer: 105
Answer & Explanation: 204

Q-144:   Which of the following is a prerequisite to the reversal of a stock posting for a completed inspection lot? Select all that apply.

A. Usage decision for inspection lot

B. Creation of material document

C. Goods movement from inspection stock to unrestricted or blocked stock

D. Activity allowed by batch status

Short Answer: 105
Answer & Explanation: 204

Q-145:   "Display List of Batches for a Material" and "Display Batch Characteristic Values" are examples of what?

A. Menu option for Usage Decision function

B. Menu option for QMIS

C. Menu option for Results Recording function

Short Answer: 105
Answer & Explanation: 205

Q-146: Which of the following is an activity that is required to reverse a stock posting? Select all that apply.

A. Create a goods receipt reversal with reference to the original purchase order using the Create/Change Inspection Lot function

B. Create return delivery with reference to the original purchase order using the Inventory Management component

C. Cancel the QM inspection lot with the QM Create/Change Inspection Lot function

Short Answer: 105
Answer & Explanation: 205

Q-147: A stock posting for a serialized material is not created as expected. What could be the problem?

A. Serial number profile is not assigned to the material

B. Material is not posted to blocked stock

C. Single units control indicator is set for material master record inspection type

Short Answer: 105
Answer & Explanation: 206

Q-148: Which of the following is used to maintain a usage decision code?

A. Catalog for Usage Decisions #6

B. Catalog for Usage Decisions #3

C. Catalog for Usage Decisions # 5

Short Answer: 105
Answer & Explanation: 207

Q-149:   Why is the batch status indicator set in an automatic proposal for a stock posting?

A. Automatic proposal for a stock posting

B. Manual confirmation of stock posting

C. Change batch status per the usage decision

Short Answer: 105
Answer & Explanation: 207

Q-150:   What is the purpose of the transfer of inspection results to the characteristics in the batch classification for a material? Select all that apply.

A. Attach the results of a quality inspection to the batch determination procedure

B. Automatically valuate the general characteristics of the class using the measurement results of the closed characteristics

C. Determine the use of individual batches according to inspection characteristics

D. Determine the batches in inspection stock

Short Answer: 105
Answer & Explanation: 208

Q-151: What is a prerequisite to the transfer of characteristic inspection results to the general characteristics to the characteristics in the batch classification? Select all that apply.

A. Material is identified as a batch material in the material master

B. The master inspection characteristics are linked to the general characteristics in the classification system

C. The batch class was assigned to the material in the classification view of the material master

D. Batch is posted to "New Material"

E. Batch is released

Short Answer: 105
Answer & Explanation: 209

Q-152: Which of the following is a valid restriction related to the change of results that have been recorded for an inspection lot?

A. Recorded results can be changed before the usage decision is entered for an inspection lot

B. Recorded results can be changed with history after a usage decision is entered for an inspection lot

C. Recorded results can be changed without history after a usage decision is entered for an inspection lot

Short Answer: 105
Answer & Explanation: 210

Q-153: What method is used to create a quality score for a inspection lot? Select all that apply.

A. Manual entry

B. Automatic entry based on Usage Decision catalog and inspection type

C. Automatic entry based on material master record inspection type and algorithm

D. Automatic entry based weighted share of defects in a lot

Short Answer: 106
Answer & Explanation: 210

Q-154: The algorithm used to calculate a quality score is defined for which of the following?

A. Inspection type

B. Usage decision code

C. Inspection lot

D. Defect class

Short Answer: 106
Answer & Explanation: 211

Q-155: Which of the following can be used to calculate a quality score that is defined for an individual inspection type? Select all that apply.

A. Defect classes

B. Inspection lot

C. Algorithm assigned to material master inspection type

D. Share of defects for characteristics

Short Answer: 106
Answer & Explanation: 211

Q-156: Identify a true statement if a quality score is based on the usage decision?

A. Quality score is assigned to group code in Usage Decision catalog

B. Quality score is derived using algorithm defined in material master inspection type

C. Inspection with plan

Short Answer: 106
Answer & Explanation: 212

Q-157: Which of the following is a requirement if a quality score is defined for an inspection type on the basis of the quality score for characteristics? Select all that apply.

A. Inspection plan is used to inspect the materials

B. Defect classes are assigned to defect codes

C. Algorithm for calculation of quality score is defined for inspection lot

Short Answer: 106
Answer & Explanation: 213

Q-158: What is the relationship between a quality score and a usage decision? Select all that apply.

A. Quality score is not related to the usage decision code but rather the quality notification

B. Quality score can be directly assigned to group code in Usage Decision catalog

C. Quality score can be calculated per algorithm defined in material master record inspection type

Short Answer: 106
Answer & Explanation: 213

Q-159: What is a valid method used to create a quality score for an inspection lot when a usage decision is entered? Select all that apply.

A. Manual procedure to enter quality score

B. Automatic procedure to enter a quality score on the basis of the material

C. Automatic procedure to enter a quality score on the basis of the inspection type and the usage decision code

Short Answer: 106
Answer & Explanation: 214

Q-160: Which of the following is a true statement regarding an automatic procedure to calculate a quality score for an inspection lot when a usage decision is entered? Select all that apply.

A. Plan must be used for inspection if quality score is derived from the usage decision code

B. A unique quality score cannot be defined for individual usage decision code

C. Quality score can be calculated with procedure or defined for usage decision code

Short Answer: 106
Answer & Explanation: 214

Q-161:   How are the upper and lower limits for a quality score are defined?

A. Usage decision transaction

B. Catalog Basic Data

C. Customizing application

Short Answer: 106
Answer & Explanation: 215

Q-162:   "Share of defects for characteristics" and "usage decision code" are examples of what?

A. Inspection Lot Completion component lists

B. Data used in calculation of a quality score for an inspection lot

C. Code group in Usage Decision catalog

Short Answer: 106
Answer & Explanation: 216

Q-163:   Which of the following is required to use the inspection lot share of defects to calculate a quality score?

A. Manual assignment of quality score

B. Algorithm to calculate quality score for material master record inspection type

C. Quality score assigned to group code in Usage Decision catalog

Short Answer: 106
Answer & Explanation: 216

Q-164:   What function leads to the confirmation of appraisal costs that are incurred due to the performance of an inspection operation? Select all that apply.

A. Complete inspection without a usage decision

B. Record usage decision

C. Complete short-term inspection

Short Answer: 107
Answer & Explanation: 217

Q-165:   How is the confirmed defective quantity for an inspection lot used? Select all that apply.

A. Creation of notification item

B. Vendor evaluation

C. Vendor letter of complaint

Short Answer: 107
Answer & Explanation: 218

Q-166:   Identify a true statement regarding a quality score. Select all that apply.

A. A quality score can be manually entered as results are recorded or as a usage decision is entered to the system

B. The procedure used to automatically calculate a quality score can be defined and activated when inspection type is activated

C. A quality score can be based on the share of defects for each characteristic or for the inspection lot

Short Answer: 107
Answer & Explanation: 219

Q-167:   Which of the following is a requirement to automatically record a usage decision? Select all that apply.

A. All inspected characteristics of the inspection lot are accepted

B. All required inspection characteristics are confirmed and closed

C. No defect records were created for the inspection lot

D. Only defect records of a minor defect class were created for the inspection lot

E. Only short-term characteristics are rejected

Short Answer: 107
Answer & Explanation: 219

Q-168:   Which of the following is a requirement to automatically record a usage decision? Select all that apply.

A. Automatic usage decision selected in material master inspection settings

B. Customizing settings for the automatic usage decision in the inspection type

C. No certificate for goods receipt requirement

D. All inspection characteristics in inspection lot are accepted

Short Answer: 107
Answer & Explanation: 220

Q-169:   You want to determine a quality score for an inspection lot. Which of the following is an input to the formula used to calculate the quality score?

A. Share of defects in lot

B. Number of defects for characteristics

C. Share of defects for material

Short Answer: 107
Answer & Explanation: 221

Q-170:   What is the purpose of the entry of a usage decision?

A. Determine inspection intervals

B. Determine if a material in an inspection lot is accepted or rejected for its intended purpose

C. Determine if an inspection should be continued

Short Answer: 107

Answer & Explanation: 221

Q-171:   An inspection is categorized as a short-term completion on what basis?

A. Required characteristics are not valuated

B. Inspection points are not valuated

C. Optional characteristics are not valuated

Short Answer: 107
Answer & Explanation: 222

Q-172:   When a usage decision is recorded, which of the following can occur?

A. Times for activity types can be confirmed to a QM order

B. Prices for activity types can be confirmed to a QM order

C. Activity costs can be confirmed to a QM order

Short Answer: 107
Answer & Explanation: 222

Q-173:   You want inspection results to be transferred to the batch class when a usage decision is entered. Where do you designate a material as a batch material?

A. Inspection type

B. Inspection lot

C. Material master record

D. Inspection characteristic

Short Answer: 107
Answer & Explanation: 223

Q-174:   What is a result of the completion of an inspection lot?

A. Quality level for current inspection lot is updated

B. Quality score for inspection characteristics if calculated

C. The recorded results for a characteristic cannot be changed

Short Answer: 107
Answer & Explanation: 224

Q-175:   What alternative exists to complete an inspection without a usage decision. Select all that apply.

A. Complete inspection with open characteristics

B. Complete inspection on short-term basis

C. Close characteristics and complete inspection

D. Discontinue inspection

Short Answer: 108
Answer & Explanation: 224

Q-176:   How do you complete an inspection if inspection points exist that have not been valuated? Select all that apply.

A. Complete inspection on a short-term basis

B. Discontinue inspection

C. Valuate inspection points and enter the usage decision

D. Complete inspection

Short Answer: 108
Answer & Explanation: 225

Q-177:   How would you access a display of the inspection points that exist for a particular inspection lot? Select all that apply.

A. Create Usage Decision function

B. Change Usage Decision function

C. Display Results function

Short Answer: 108
Answer & Explanation: 226

Q-178:   The transaction Overview of Inspection Points identifies inspection points for inspection lots for which of the following? Select all that apply.

A. Production quantities

B. Physical samples

C. Equipment

Short Answer: 108
Answer & Explanation: 226

Q-179: Which of the following is required to enter a usage decision? Select all that apply.

A. Results recorded for all required inspection characteristics

B. Receipt of required quality certificate

C. Active status inspection lot

D. Inspector authorization to make usage decision

Short Answer: 108
Answer & Explanation: 227

Q-180: The system does not allow the manual entry of a usage decision for an inspection lot. What do you check in this instance? Select all that apply.

A. Active status of inspection lot

B. Entry of inspection results for optional characteristics

C. Usage Decision function authorization

D. Release of inspection lot

Short Answer: 108
Answer & Explanation: 228

Q-181: What statement is correct regarding a usage decision?

A. Quality notification can't be activated prior to entry of usage decision

B. All inspection results must be recorded for all required characteristics prior to entry of usage decision

C. Receipt of quality certificate must be confirmed prior to entry of usage decision

Short Answer: 108
Answer & Explanation: 228

Q-182:   The customer wants to view defects recorded for an operation rather than for a characteristic. What Inspection Lot Completion component function will enable him to do so?

A. Usage Decision - Display Defect Structure

B. Usage Decision - Overview of Characteristics

C. Logistics Evaluations - Inspection Results

Short Answer: 108
Answer & Explanation: 229

Q-183:   The customer wants to view the defects that were recorded at the operations defect recording level for a particular inspection lot. How should he do so?

A. Usage Decision - Display Defects list

B. Usage Decision - Display Defect Structure

C. Usage Decision - Display Results for Characteristics

Short Answer: 108
Answer & Explanation: 230

Q-184: When an automatic stock posting occurs, how is the account determined?

A. Batch status control indicator for usage decision code

B. Background processing control indicator for usage decision code

C. Stock proposal control indicator for usage decision code

Short Answer: 108
Answer & Explanation: 230

Q-185: How would you display all the stock postings for an inspection lot using an Inspection Lot Completion function?

A. Usage Decision - Overview of Stocks

B. Usage Decision - List of Materials for Inspection Lot

C. Usage Decision - Display Inspection Lot

Short Answer: 108
Answer & Explanation: 231

Q-186: Identify a prerequisite to the confirmation of values for activity types to a QM order as inspection results are recorded or the usage decision is entered. Select all that apply.

A. Assignment of QM order to inspection lot

B. Assignment of QM order to inspection type

C. Assignment of QM order to a material

Short Answer: 108
Answer & Explanation: 231

Q-187: What is required for the system to automatically calculate the quantity of material that is destroyed in an inspection and post this quantity to sample usage?

A. Destructive inspection for characteristic control indicator

B. Destructive inspection for inspection type control indicator

C. Destructive inspection for inspection operation control indicator

Short Answer: 108
Answer & Explanation: 232

Q-188: At what point are times confirmed to a QM order for activity types? Select all that apply.

A. Results recording process

B. Usage decision process

C. Defects recording process

D. All of the above

E. None of the above

Short Answer: 109
Answer & Explanation: 233

Q-189:   What is the result of the transfer of the usage decision code and quality score for an inspection lot to the characteristics in the batch classification for a material when a usage decision is entered for the lot?

A. Batch classification data will be displayed in the usage decision log

B. Batch classification data will be displayed in the usage decision data in a follow-up action e-mail

C.   Object link is created between batch class and workflow work items

Short Answer: 109
Answer & Explanation: 233

Q-190:   The automatic transfer of inspection results to characteristics in a batch classification for a material is triggered by what?

A. Usage Decision function

B. Results Recording function

C. Defects Recording function

Short Answer: 109
Answer & Explanation: 234

Q-191:   Activity confirmations for operations enable you to confirm values for activity types to a QM order. Which of the following can be performed when you change a usage decision?

A. Display a cost report

B. Create a QM order

C. Enter activity types

Short Answer: 109
Answer & Explanation: 235

Q-192:   At what organization level are the upper and lower limits defined for a quality score?

A. Client

B. Plant

Short Answer: 109
Answer & Explanation: 235

Q-193:   Which of the following triggers an automatic proposal for a stock posting?

A. Defect code

B. Usage decision code

C. Task code

Short Answer: 109
Answer & Explanation: 236

Q-194:   How can the customer determine the characteristics that are relevant for a particular usage decision for an inspection lot?

A. Results Recording - Results History

B. Usage Decision - Characteristics tab

C. Usage Decision - Results History

D. Results Recording - Characteristics tab

Q-195:   Which of the following is a valid function of the Inspection Lot Completion component? Select all that apply.

A. Display Quantity of Units Rejected in Inspection Lot

B. Change Inspection Lot Status

C. Record Usage Decision

D. Confirm Activities for Operations

E. Record Quality Score (with manual procedure)

Short Answer: 109
Answer & Explanation: 237

Q-196:   What is the purpose of confirming activities for inspection operations? Select all that apply.

A. Track the appraisal costs incurred at a work center for activities performed in an operation

B. Confirm times for activity types to a QM order when inspection results or usage decision is recorded

C. Monitor and analyze costs that originate in corporate-wide operations

D. Track nonconformity costs incurred at plant for activities performed in operation

Short Answer: 109

Answer & Explanation: 237

Q-197:   What is required to reverse a stock posting?

A. Material in inspection lot has been posted from inspection stock to unrestricted stock

B. Usage decision has been recorded for inspection characteristics

C. Inspection lot is cancelled

Short Answer: 109
Answer & Explanation: 238

Q-198:   The user would like to review stock transfers between storage locations, as well as stock postings that occurred simultaneously with the usage decision. What is used to accommodate this request?

A. Material document

B. List of material documents for inspection lots

C. Goods receipt document

Short Answer: 109
Answer & Explanation: 238

Q-199:   What is the purpose of the list of material documents for a stock-relevant inspection lot? Select all that apply.

A. Display stock posted at the creation of the inspection lot

B. Display stock transfers between work centers

C. Display stock posted with Results Recording function

Short Answer: 109
Answer & Explanation: 239

Q-200:   The user would like to review the material documents that were created as a result of a stock posting. What is used to accommodate this request?

A. Usage Decision - Overview of Stocks

B. Inspection Lot Completion - Overview of Stocks

C. Results Recording - Overview of Stocks

Short Answer: 109
Answer & Explanation: 239

Q-201:   What would you use to display the inspection results for more than one inspection lot?

A. Results Recording - Results History

B. Evaluations – QMIS

C. Usage Decision - Characteristics tab

Short Answer: 109
Answer & Explanation: 240

CHAPTER II

SHORT ANSWERS

SHORT ANSWERS

Q-1:   C. Calculate quality score for inspection lot

Q-2:   B. Activate quality notification, C. Record stock posting and E. Determine defective quantity for an inspection type

Q-3:   B. Automatic functions performed at the entry of a usage decision for the inspection lot

Q-4:   C. Customizing application is used to create follow-up actions

Q-5:   B. Usage Decision

Q-6:   A. Complete the inspection without a usage decision and with open characteristics, B. Complete the inspection without a usage decision and with closed characteristics and C. Complete short-term inspection

Q-7:   A. Stock proposal control indicator in catalog type 3 set code and B. Background processing control indicator in catalog type 3 set code

Q-8:   C. Worklist function

Q-9:   A. Stock proposal control indicator in catalog type 3 set code and B. Background processing control indicator in catalog type 3 set code

Q-10:   B. Material

Q-11:   B. Results recording and C. Usage decision

Q-12: A. Release of inspection lot and B. Valuation of required inspection characteristics defined for inspection lot

Q-13: A. A required certificate must be received prior to the entry of usage decision and B. Usage decision can be made irrespective of unevaluated inspection points

Q-14: B. ACDB

Q-15: B. Inspection lot status is "Released" and D. User is granted authorization for transaction

Q-16: B. Usage Decision

Q-17: D. Any of the above

Q-18: C. Usage Decision function – Display Related Notification

Q-19: B. User authorization to enter usage decision

Q-20: C. Usage Decision function – Display Related Notifications

Q-21: C. Maintenance notification

Q-22: A. Update to inspection lot status to reflect status of follow-up action

Q-23: B. Select the Evaluation tab in the Logistics QM Information System menu

Q-24: A. Usage Decision function – Overview of Stocks

Q-25: B. Equipment and C. Functional location

Q-26: A. Enter usage decision, B. Discontinue inspection and C. Valuate inspection points and enter usage decision

Q-27: A. Usage Decision – Overview of Stocks

Q-28: D. Material document

Q-29: C. Usage Decision

Q-30: A. Usage Decision

Q-31: C. Usage Decision

Q-32: B. Usage Decision – Material Documents

Q-33: A. Create transfer posting from blocked stock to unrestricted use stock in Quality Management and C. Create return delivery for purchase order in Inventory Management

Q-34: A. Create list of defect records created for inspection lot, B. Identify defect types documented in defect records for an inspection lot and C. Activate quality notifications on the basis of the defect class of the defect code

Q-35: A. Program executed with job management function

Q-36: B. The four units can be posted to unrestricted use stock as a group and one object list can be assigned to the individual material document(s)

Q-37: A. No inspection lot characteristic was rejected in the inspection lot and C. Defect records were created for critical defects and activated as notifications during the inspection

Q-38:   B. Usage decision code

Q-39:   A. Enter the usage decision for the inspection lot

Q-40:   C. Enter stock posting after the entry of a usage decision for an inspection lot

Q-41:   B. Material is destroyed in an inspection

Q-42:   A. Sample usage and B. Return delivery

Q-43:   B. Control indicator in usage decision code

Q-44:   A. Control indicator in usage decision code

Q-45:   C. Usage Decision

Q-46:   D. The "no change to batch status" control indicator was set in the set code

Q-47:   B. Results Recording and C. Usage Decision

Q-48:   D. Stock proposal control indicator in the usage decision code

Q-49:   B. Characteristic

Q-50:   A. Destructive inspection control indicator in the inspection characteristic

Q-51:   B. Batch status control indicator in the catalog type 3 code

Q-52:   B. Usage Decision

Q-53: A. The documents in the list account for the original stock posting for the creation of a stock-relevant inspection lot and B. The documents in the list account for a decrease to the original stock in an inspection lot

Q-54: A. Inspection lot

Q-55: C. Usage Decision

Q-56: A. Display Material Documents for Inspection Lots and B. Record Defective Quantity

Q-57: B. Stock account for stock destroyed in quality inspection

Q-58: A. Destructive inspection for inspection characteristic control indicator and B. Stock proposal control indicator for usage decision set code

Q-59: A. Stock proposal indicator for usage decision code and B. Background processing indicator for usage decision code

Q-60: B. Stock proposal control indicator for usage decision set code and C. Background processing control indicator for usage decision code

Q-61: B. Stock proposal control indicator for usage decision set code and C. Background processing control indicator for usage decision code

Q-62: A. Usage Decision

Q-63: C. Background processing control indicator in usage decision set code

Q-64: D. Any of the above

Q-65: A. Release of the inspection lot and B. Authorization of the user to enter the usage decision for the inspection lot

Q-66: A. Stock posting before, during or after usage decision and C. Stock account to which material should be posted from an inspection lot

Q-67: B. Usage Decision

Q-68: A. Usage Decision: Overview of Defects

Q-69: A. Inspection results can be changed for an inspection lot unless the inspection is completed without a usage decision and B. Inspection results can be entered for the inspection lot after it is completed on a short-term basis

Q-70: B. Date of stock posting

Q-71: B. Usage Decision

Q-72: A. Material in inspection lot was posted to blocked stock

Q-73: E. None of the Above

Q-74: B. Inspection lot number

Q-75: D. All of the above

Q-76:   B. Complete Inspection on Short-term Basis and D. Create Usage Decision

Q-77:   A. Reverse Stock Posting

Q-78:   A. Confirm the receipt of a certificate and C. Display defect structure

Q-79:   A. Determine the types of defects confirmed for an inspection lot and C. Determine the hierarchical level at which defect records were created

Q-80:   B. Share of defects in inspection lot and C. Share of defects for characteristics

Q-81:   D. Usage decision for the inspection lot

Q-82:   A. Calculate quality score for the inspection lot, C. Trigger follow-up actions and D. Update quality level

Q-83:   A. Batches, C. Catalogs and E. Inspection Lot Creation

Q-84:   A. Usage Decision - Defect Structure

Q-85:   A. Usage decision code

Q-86:   B. Display defect structure

Q-87:   C. Usage Decision

Q-88:   A. Inspection type

Q-89:   B. Results Recording and C. Usage Decision

Q-90:   A. Activate quality notification, D. Create stock posting and E. Confirm activities for inspection operation

Q-91:   C. Usage Decision

Q-92:   A. Create defect record and C. Confirm activities for inspection operation

Q-93:   A. Recorded results cannot be changed subsequent to documentation of usage decision

Q-94:   A. Recorded results for required inspection characteristics

Q-95:   B. Results recorded for required inspection characteristics and C. Authorization to record usage decision

Q-96:   B. Inspection type

Q-97:   A. Sample size and B. Acceptance number

Q-98:   A. Required characteristics must be closed prior to entry of the usage decision

Q-99:   A. Create stock posting

Q-100: D. Overview of Stocks

Q-101: A. Usage Decision - Overview of Characteristics

Q-102: A. Overview of Characteristics, B. Overview of Defects and C. Overview of Stocks

Q-103: A. True

Q-104: C. Usage Decision – Overview of Defects

Q-105: B. Overview of Stocks and C. Overview of Defects

Q-106: A. Usage Decision – Overview of Defects

Q-107: B. Usage Decision

Q-108: D. Post a quantity of material to a particular stock type

Q-109: A. Reset status of the inspection lot

Q-110: C. Discontinue the inspection

Q-111: C. Authorization to make usage decision

Q-112: C. Results have been recorded for required characteristics

Q-113: A. Confirmation of the receipt of a quality certificate, C. Release of inspection lot and D. User authorization for the transaction

Q-114: A. Status of the inspection lot is "Released" and C. Authorization to enter the usage decision

Q-115: B. It is not necessary to record all inspection results for required inspection characteristics for the inspection lot prior to the entry of the usage decision

Q-116: A. Usage Decision - Overview of Defects

Q-117: B. The defects recorded for an inspection lot

Q-118: A. Usage Decision – Overview of Defects

Q-119: C. Usage Decision

Q-120: C. Initiate corrective action

Q-121: B. Entry of usage decision code

Q-122: A. Quality score is calculated, C. Inspection lot status is updated and D. Subsequent entries to record inspection results can be made

Q-123: B. Background processing control indicator for the usage decision code and C. Stock proposal control indicator for the usage decision code

Q-124: B. Overview of Characteristics

Q-125: B. Activate quality notification

Q-126: B. Overview of Characteristics

Q-127: B. Display the inspection results for a characteristic in the inspection lot

Q-128: B. Display inspection results for a characteristic in chronological order

Q-129: D. All of the above

Q-130: B. Stock posting to scrap and C. Stock posting to blocked stock

Q-131: A. A manual or automatic process is used to make the stock posting and B. Postings in the

Material Management component are made
on the basis of stock postings entered in QM

Q-132: B. Inspection lot that is created with a manual
process

Q-133: B. Usage Decision Results History

Q-134: A. Inspection lot quantity correction and B.
Stock transfer

Q-135: A. Stock proposal control indicator for usage
decision code and B. Background processing
control indicator for usage decision code

Q-136: C. Usage decision set code

Q-137: A. Goods receipt document and B. Material
document

Q-138: A. Inspection lot number and C. Quantity of
stock to be posted

Q-139: A. Ability to post stock for one inspection lot
versus multiple inspection lots and B. Manual
entry of stock posting versus use of worklist
to post stocks

Q-140: A. Batch display, B. Batch where-used list and
C. Post batch to new material

Q-141: A. Creation of a serial number profile for
movement type and B. Selection of single-unit
inspection using serial numbers control
indicator for material master inspection type

Q-142: D. All of the above

Q-143:   C. Inspection lot record

Q-144:   A. Usage decision for inspection lot and C. Goods movement from inspection stock to unrestricted or blocked stock

Q-145:   A. Menu option for Usage Decision function

Q-146:   B. Create return delivery with reference to the original purchase order using the Inventory Management component

Q-147:   A. Serial number profile is not assigned to the material

Q-148:   B. Catalog for Usage Decisions #3

Q-149:   C. Change batch status per the usage decision

Q-150:   A. Attach the results of a quality inspection to the batch determination procedure and B. Automatically valuate the general characteristics of the class using the measurement results of the closed characteristics

Q-151:   A. Material is identified as a batch material in the material master, B. The master inspection characteristics are linked to the general characteristics in the classification system and C. The batch class was assigned to the material in the classification view of the material master

Q-152:   A. Recorded results can be changed before the usage decision is entered for an inspection lot

Q-153:   A. Manual entry and C. Automatic entry based on material master record inspection type and algorithm

Q-154:   A. Inspection type

Q-155:   C. Algorithm assigned to material master inspection type and D. Share of defects for characteristics

Q-156:   B. Quality score is derived using algorithm defined in material master inspection type

Q-157:   A. Inspection plan is used to inspect the materials and B. Defect classes are assigned to defect codes

Q-158:   C. Quality score can be calculated per algorithm defined in material master record inspection type

Q-159:   A. Manual procedure to enter quality score and C. Automatic procedure to enter a quality score on the basis of the inspection type and the usage decision code

Q-160:   C. Quality score can be calculated with procedure or defined for usage decision code

Q-161:   C. Customizing application

Q-162:   B. Data used in calculation of a quality score for an inspection lot

Q-163:   B. Algorithm to calculate quality score for material master record inspection type and C. Quality score assigned to group code in Usage Decision catalog

Q-164:   B. Record usage decision

Q-165:   B. Vendor evaluation and C. Vendor letter of complaint

Q-166:   B. The procedure used to automatically calculate a quality score can be defined and activated when inspection type is activated and C. A quality score can be based on the share of defects for each characteristic or for the inspection lot

Q-167:   A. All inspected characteristics of the inspection lot are accepted, B. All required inspection characteristics are confirmed and closed and C. No defect records were created for the inspection lot

Q-168:   D. All inspection characteristics in inspection lot are accepted

Q-169:   A. Share of defects in lot

Q-170:   B. Determine if a material in an inspection lot is accepted or rejected for its intended purpose

Q-171:   A. Required characteristics are not valuated

Q-172:   A. Times for activity types can be confirmed to a QM order

Q-173:   C. Material master record

Q-174:   A. Quality level for current inspection lot is updated and C. The recorded results for a characteristic cannot be changed

Q-175: A. Complete inspection with open characteristics and B. Complete inspection on short-term basis

Q-176: B. Discontinue inspection and C. Valuate the inspection points and enter usage decision

Q-177: A. Create Usage Decision function and B. Change Usage Decision function

Q-178: A. Production quantities, B. Physical samples and C. Equipment

Q-179: A. Results recorded for all required inspection characteristics and B. Receipt of required quality certificate

Q-180: C. Usage Decision function authorization and D. Release of inspection lot

Q-181: C. Receipt of quality certificate must be confirmed prior to entry of usage decision

Q-182: A. Usage Decision - Display Defect Structure

Q-183: B. Usage Decision – Display Defect Structure

Q-184: C. Stock proposal control indicator for usage decision code

Q-185: A. Usage Decision – Overview of Stocks

Q-186: C. Assignment of QM order to a material

Q-187: A. Destructive inspection for characteristic control indicator

Q-188: A. Results recording process and B. Usage decision process

Q-189: A. Batch classification data will be displayed in the usage decision log

Q-190: A. Usage Decision function

Q-191: A. Display a cost report

Q-192: A. Client

Q-193: B. Usage decision code

Q-194: B. Usage Decision – Characteristics tab

Q-195: C. Record Usage Decision and D. Confirm Activities for Operations

Q-196: A. Track the appraisal costs incurred at a work center for activities performed in an operation and B. Confirm times for activity types to a QM order when inspection results or usage decision is recorded

Q-197: A. Material in inspection lot has been posted from inspection stock to unrestricted stock

Q-198: B. List of material documents for inspection lots

Q-199: A. Display stock posted at the creation of inspection lot

Q-200: A. Usage Decision – Overview of Stocks

Q-201: B. Evaluations - QMIS

CHAPTER III

ANSWERS & EXPLANATIONS

ANSWERS & EXPLANATIONS

Q-1:   C. Calculate quality score for inspection lot

A quality inspection is conducted to confirm the acceptability of a product for its intended purpose. During the inspection process, the results for inspection characteristics are recorded and compared with predefined quality requirements. On the basis of this comparison, individual characteristics are accepted or rejected. At the conclusion of the inspection, on the basis of inspection characteristic valuations, a usage decision is documented for the inspection lot. As the usage decision is documented, other functions are automatically performed by the system. For example, a quality score for the inspection lot is calculated and a quality level data record, which determines inspection stages for a subsequent inspection lot, is updated. In addition, the Quality Management Information System is updated and follow-up actions are executed.

Q-2:   B. Activate quality notification, C. Record stock posting and E. Determine defective quantity for an inspection type

A quality inspection is conducted to confirm the acceptability of a product for its intended purpose. During the inspection process, the results for inspection characteristics are recorded and compared with predefined quality requirements. On the basis of this comparison, individual characteristics are accepted or rejected. At the conclusion of the inspection, on the basis of inspection characteristic valuations, a usage decision is documented for the inspection lot. As the usage decision is documented, other functions are automatically performed by the system. For example, a quality score for the inspection lot is calculated and a quality level data record, which determines inspection stages for a subsequent inspection lot, is updated. Also, the Quality Management Information System is updated and follow-up actions are executed. In addition to the automatic functions, the user may elect to perform other functions, as well. For example, the user can create defect records, activate quality notifications, create stock postings and confirm activities for quality orders.

Q-3:   B. Automatic functions performed at the entry of a usage decision for the inspection lot

A quality inspection is conducted to confirm the acceptability of a product for its intended purpose. During the inspection process, the results for inspection characteristics are recorded and compared with predefined quality requirements. On the basis of this comparison, individual characteristics are accepted or rejected. At the conclusion of the inspection, on the basis of inspection characteristic valuations, a usage decision is documented for the inspection lot. As the usage decision is documented, other functions are automatically performed by the system. For example, a quality score for the inspection lot is calculated and a quality level data record, which determines inspection stages for a subsequent inspection lot, is updated. In addition, the Quality Management Information System is updated and follow-up actions are executed.

Q-4:   C. Customizing application is used to create follow-up actions

A quality inspection is conducted to confirm the acceptability of a product for its intended purpose. During the inspection process, the results for inspection characteristics are recorded and compared with predefined quality requirements. On the basis of this comparison, individual characteristics are accepted

or rejected. At the conclusion of the inspection, on the basis of inspection characteristic valuations, a usage decision is documented for the inspection lot. As the usage decision is documented, other functions are automatically performed by the system. For example, a quality score for the inspection lot is calculated and a quality level data record, which determines inspection stages for a subsequent inspection lot, is updated. In addition, the Quality Management Information System is updated and follow-up actions are executed. The follow-up actions can be maintained with the Customizing application.

Q-5:   B. Usage Decision

A quality inspection is conducted to confirm the acceptability of a product for its intended purpose. During the inspection process, the results for inspection characteristics are recorded and compared with predefined quality requirements. On the basis of this comparison, individual characteristics are accepted or rejected. At the conclusion of the inspection, on the basis of inspection characteristic valuations, a usage decision is documented for the inspection lot. As the usage decision is documented, other functions are automatically performed by the system. For example, a quality score for the inspection lot is calculated and a quality level data record, which determines inspection stages for a subsequent inspection lot, is updated. In addition, the Quality Management Information System is updated and follow-up actions are executed. In addition to the automatic functions, the user may elect to perform other functions, as well. For example, the user can create defect records, activate quality notifications, create stock postings and confirm activities for quality orders.

Q-6:   A. Complete the inspection without a usage decision and with open characteristics, B. Complete the inspection without a usage decision and with closed characteristics and C. Complete short-term inspection

A quality inspection is conducted to confirm the acceptability of a product for its intended purpose. During the inspection process, the results for inspection characteristics are recorded and compared with predefined quality requirements. On the basis of this comparison, individual characteristics are accepted or rejected. At the conclusion of the inspection, on the basis of inspection characteristic valuations, a usage decision is documented for the inspection lot. The entry of the usage decision typically requires the closure of all required characteristics and processed optional characteristics. However, it may be necessary to complete an inspection even if all inspection results have not been recorded for some required characteristics or some processed optional characteristics. In this case, the user has two options. The inspection can be completed with the Usage Decision - Complete Inspection function. In this instance, the status of the inspection lot is changed to "close completed." As an alternative, the short-term characteristics can be closed by changing the status of the inspection lot to "short-term inspection completed" with the Usage Decision – Short-term Inspection function. In both cases, inspection results may not be revised unless the inspection lot status is reset.

Q-7:   A. Stock proposal control indicator in catalog type 3 set code and B. Background processing control indicator in catalog type 3 set code

A stock posting documents the entry or removal of a manufactured or procured material to or from stock. The posting ensures that the material in a stock-relevant inspection lot is properly accounted for, which contributes to effective logistics management and financial propriety. The Inspection Lot Completion component includes the functionality necessary to display stock that has been posted to or from a particular inspection lot and to make additional stock postings. For example, as a usage decision for a material is recorded, the system automatically proposes a stock account to which the material can be posted. The stock account is proposed according to control indicators that are set for the usage decision codes. The stock proposal function requires the selection of the stock proposal control indicator in catalog type 3 set code and the background processing control indicator in catalog type 3 set code. The usage decision codes can be defined for a selected set that, in turn, is defined for an inspection type or for the inspection catalog type 3.

Q-8: C. Worklist function

At the conclusion of an inspection, on the basis of the valuation of individual inspection characteristics, the Usage Decision function is used to document the acceptance or disapproval of the inspection lot for its intended purpose. In turn, usage decisions for multiple inspection lots can be recorded simultaneously with the Worklist function. To use the Worklist function, the user must enter selection criteria, with which the system selects the inspection lots it will process simultaneously. The selected inspection lots are then displayed in a worklist from which the user selects one or more lots and enters the usage decisions for each of the selected lots, one after the other.

Q-9: A. Stock proposal control indicator in catalog type 3 set code and B. Background processing control indicator in catalog type 3 set code

A stock posting documents the entry or removal of a manufactured or procured material to or from stock. The posting ensures that the material in a stock-relevant inspection lot is properly accounted for, which

contributes to effective logistics management and financial propriety. The Inspection Lot Completion component includes the functionality necessary to display stock that has been posted to or from a particular inspection lot and to make additional stock postings. For example, as a usage decision for a material is recorded, the system automatically proposes a stock account to which the material can be posted. The stock account is proposed according to control indicators that are set for the usage decision codes. The stock proposal function requires the selection of the stock proposal control indicator in catalog type 3 set code and the background processing control indicator in catalog type 3 set code. The usage decision codes can be defined for a selected set that, in turn, is defined for an inspection type or for the inspection catalog type 3.

Q-10:   B. Material

Quality Management orders are used to collect and manage quality costs that are incurred in the performance of QM activities. The orders are the means by which activities that support the processing of quality inspections are linked to cost assignment objects in the Controlling component. To capture appraisal costs that originate with a particular inspection lot, a QM order is created when the inspection lot is created, the order is assigned to a material and/or inspection lot. Next, quality costs, in the form of activity times, are assigned to activity types and subsequently confirmed to a QM order. Then, the confirmed activities are settled to the appropriate cost assignment object(s) in the Controlling component.

Q-11:   B. Results Recording and C. Usage Decision

Quality Management orders are used to collect and manage quality costs that are incurred in the performance of QM activities. The orders are the means by which activities that support the processing of quality inspections are linked to cost assignment objects in the Controlling component. To capture appraisal costs, a QM order is created when the inspection lot is created and assigned to a material and or and inspection lot. Next, quality costs, in the form of activity times, are assigned to activity types and confirmed to a QM order and settled to the appropriate cost assignment object in the Controlling component. Both the Results Recording and Usage Decision functions can be used to confirm inspection activities.

Q-12:   A. Release of inspection lot and B. Valuation of required inspection characteristics defined for inspection lot

A quality inspection is conducted to confirm the acceptability of a product for its intended purpose. During the inspection process, the results for inspection characteristics are recorded and compared with predefined quality requirements. On the basis of this comparison, individual characteristics are accepted or rejected. At the conclusion of the inspection, on the basis of inspection characteristic valuations, a usage decision is documented for the inspection lot. The entry of a usage decision for the inspection lot requires the documentation of inspection results for all required characteristics and processed optional characteristics, and the valuation of characteristics. In addition, the inspection lot must be released, the status of the inspection lot must permit the entry of the usage decision, the user must be authorized to execute the Usage Decision function and any required certificate must have been received. The usage decision for the inspection lot can be recorded irrespective of unevaluated inspection points.

Q-13:   A. A required certificate must be received prior to the entry of usage decision and B. Usage decision can be made irrespective of unevaluated inspection points

A quality inspection is conducted to confirm the acceptability of a product for its intended purpose. During the inspection process, the results for inspection characteristics are recorded and compared with predefined quality requirements. On the basis of this comparison, individual characteristics are accepted or rejected. At the conclusion of the inspection, on the basis of inspection characteristic valuations, a usage decision is documented for the inspection lot. The entry of a usage decision for the inspection lot requires the documentation of inspection results for all required characteristics and processed optional characteristics, and the valuation of characteristics. In addition, the inspection lot must be released, the status of the inspection lot must permit the entry of the usage decision, the user must be authorized to execute the Usage Decision function and any required certificate must have been received. The usage decision for the inspection lot can be recorded irrespective of unevaluated inspection points.

Q-14:   B. ACDB

A stock posting documents the entry or removal of a manufactured or procured material to or from stock. The stock posting ensures that the material in a stock-relevant inspection lot is properly accounted for, which contributes to effective logistics management and financial propriety. The Inspection Lot Completion component includes the functions necessary to make stock postings. For example, as a usage decision is recorded, the system can automatically propose a stock account to which the material in an inspection lot may be posted. The stock account is proposed according to control indicators that are set for usage decision codes, which are recorded at the conclusion of the quality inspection. In the event that a stock posting was made in error, it can be reversed. To do so requires the original entry of a usage decision for an inspection lot, a stock posting for the transfer of stock from inspection stock to unrestricted use stock, the creation of a return delivery with reference to the original purchase order and the cancellation of the inspection lot.

Q-15:   B. Inspection lot status is "Released" and D. User is granted authorization for transaction

A quality inspection is conducted to confirm the acceptability of a product for its intended purpose. During the inspection process, the results for inspection characteristics are recorded and compared with predefined quality requirements. On the basis of this comparison, individual characteristics are accepted or rejected. At the conclusion of the inspection, on the basis of inspection characteristic valuations, a usage decision is documented for the inspection lot. The entry of a usage decision for the inspection lot requires the documentation of inspection results for all required characteristics and processed optional characteristics, and the valuation of characteristics. In addition, the inspection lot must be released, the status of the inspection lot must permit the entry of the usage decision, the user must be authorized to execute the Usage Decision function and any required certificate must have been received. The usage decision for the inspection lot can be recorded irrespective of unevaluated inspection points.

Q-16:   B. Usage Decision

A quality inspection is conducted to confirm the acceptability of a product for its intended purpose. During the inspection process, the results for

inspection characteristics are recorded and compared with predefined quality requirements. On the basis of this comparison, individual characteristics are accepted or rejected. At the conclusion of the inspection, on the basis of inspection characteristic valuations, a usage decision is documented for the inspection lot. The Usage Decision function can be used to valuate inspection points and document a usage decision for an inspection lot.

Q-17:   D. Any of the above

A quality inspection is conducted to confirm the acceptability of a product for its intended purpose. During the inspection process, the results for inspection characteristics are recorded and compared with predefined quality requirements. On the basis of this comparison, individual characteristics are accepted or rejected. At the conclusion of the inspection, on the basis of inspection characteristic valuations, a usage decision is documented for the inspection lot. Typically, the entry of a usage decision for the inspection lot requires the documentation of inspection results for all required characteristics and processed optional characteristics, and the valuation of characteristics. In addition, the inspection lot must be released, the status of the inspection lot must permit the entry of the usage decision, the user must be authorized to execute the Usage Decision function and any required certificate must have been received. However, the usage decision for the inspection lot can be recorded irrespective of unevaluated inspection points. In this case, the user has two options. The inspection can be completed with the Usage Decision - Complete Inspection function. In this instance, the status of the inspection lot is changed to "close completed." As an alternative, the short-term characteristics can be closed by changing the status of the inspection lot to "short-term inspection completed" with the Usage Decision – Short-term Inspection function. In both cases, inspection results may not be revised unless the inspection lot status is reset.

Q-18:   C. Usage Decision function – Display Related Notifications

A quality inspection is conducted to confirm the acceptability of a product for its intended purpose. During the inspection process, the results for inspection characteristics are recorded and compared with predefined quality requirements. On the basis of this comparison, individual characteristics are accepted or rejected. At the conclusion of the inspection, on the basis of inspection characteristic valuations, a usage decision is documented for the inspection lot. As the usage decision is documented, other functions are automatically performed by the system. For example, a quality score for the inspection lot is calculated and a quality level data record, which determines inspection stages for a subsequent inspection lot, is updated. Also, the Quality Management Information System is updated and follow-up actions are executed. In addition to the automatic functions, the user may elect to perform other functions, as well. For example, the user can create defect records, create stock postings, confirm activities for quality orders and activate inactive quality notifications that were created to document a critical defect. To determine if all notifications have been activated that should have been activated, the Usage Decision – Display Related Notifications function can be used.

Q-19:   B. User authorization to enter usage decision

A quality inspection is conducted to confirm the acceptability of a product for its intended purpose. During the inspection process, the results for inspection characteristics are recorded and compared

with predefined quality requirements. On the basis of this comparison, individual characteristics are accepted or rejected. At the conclusion of the inspection, on the basis of inspection characteristic valuations, a usage decision is documented for the inspection lot. The entry of a usage decision for the inspection lot requires the documentation of inspection results for all required characteristics and processed optional characteristics, and the valuation of characteristics. In addition, the inspection lot must be released, the status of the inspection lot must permit the entry of the usage decision, the user must be authorized to execute the Usage Decision function and any required certificate must have been received.

Q-20:   C. Usage Decision function - Display Related Notifications

A quality inspection is conducted to confirm the acceptability of a product for its intended purpose. During the inspection process, the results for inspection characteristics are recorded and compared with predefined quality requirements. On the basis of this comparison, individual characteristics are accepted or rejected. At the conclusion of the inspection, on the basis of inspection characteristic valuations, a usage decision is documented for the inspection lot. As the usage decision is documented, other functions are automatically performed by the system. For example, a quality score for the inspection lot is calculated and a quality level data record, which determines inspection stages for a subsequent inspection lot, is updated. Also, the Quality Management Information System is updated and follow-up actions are executed. In addition to the automatic functions, the user may elect to perform other functions, as well. For example, the user can create defect records, create stock postings, confirm activities for quality orders and activate inactive quality notifications that were created to document a critical defect. To determine if all notifications have been activated that should have been activated, the Usage Decision – Display Related Notifications function can be used.

Q-21:   C. Maintenance notification

A quality inspection is conducted to confirm the acceptability of a product for its intended purpose. During the inspection process, the results for inspection characteristics are recorded and compared with predefined quality requirements. On the basis of this comparison, individual characteristics are accepted or rejected. At the conclusion of the inspection, on the basis of inspection characteristic valuations, a usage decision is documented for the inspection lot. As the usage decision is documented, other functions are automatically performed by the system. For example, a quality score for the inspection lot is calculated and a quality level data record, which determines inspection stages for a subsequent inspection lot, is updated. Also, the Quality Management Information System is updated and follow-up actions are executed. In addition to the automatic functions, the user may elect to perform other functions, as well. For example, the user can create defect records, create stock postings, confirm activities for quality orders and activate inactive quality notifications that were created to document a critical defect.

Q-22:   A. Update to inspection lot status to reflect status of follow-up action

A quality inspection is conducted to confirm the acceptability of a product for its intended purpose. During the inspection process, the results for inspection characteristics are recorded and compared with predefined quality requirements. On the basis of

this comparison, individual characteristics are accepted or rejected. At the conclusion of the inspection, on the basis of inspection characteristic valuations, a usage decision is documented for the inspection lot. As the usage decision is documented, other functions are automatically performed by the system. For example, a quality score for the inspection lot is calculated and a quality level data record, which determines inspection stages for a subsequent inspection lot, is updated. Also, the Quality Management Information System is updated and follow-up actions are executed. In addition to the automatic functions, the user may elect to perform other functions, as well. For example, the user can create defect records, create stock postings, confirm activities for quality orders and activate inactive quality notifications that were created to document a critical defect. The creation of a follow-up action triggers an update to the inspection lot status that reflects the status of the follow-up action.

Q-23:   B. Select the Evaluations tab in the Logistics QM Information System menu

A quality inspection is conducted to confirm the acceptability of a product for its intended purpose. During the inspection process, the results for inspection characteristics are recorded and compared with predefined quality requirements. On the basis of this comparison, individual characteristics are accepted or rejected. At the conclusion of the inspection, on the basis of inspection characteristic valuations, a usage decision is documented for the inspection lot. Following the valuation of characteristics, the user can view the documented inspection results for the characteristics prior to documenting the usage decision for an inspection lot. To do so, the evaluation tab in the logistics QM Information Systems screen is used.

Q-24:   A. Usage Decision function - Overview of Stocks

A stock posting documents the entry or removal of a manufactured or procured material to or from stock. The stock posting ensures that the material in a stock-relevant inspection lot is properly accounted for, which contributes to effective logistics management and financial propriety. The Inspection Lot Completion component includes the functionality necessary to view stock in the inspection lot and then post the inspected materials to the appropriate stock account. The Usage Decision – Overview of Stocks is used for this purpose.

Q-25:   B. Equipment and C. Functional location

An inspection lot may include inspection points, each of which are valuated after inspection results are recorded for each inspection point. An inspection point is a reference object assigned to an inspection operation and used to record inspection results. Each inspection point may relate to an equipment number, functional location, physical sample or production quantity. The use of inspection points allows you to conduct multiple inspections and record a separate set of characteristics for each inspection.

Q-26:   A. Enter usage decision, B. Discontinue inspection and C. Valuate inspection points and document usage decision

A quality inspection is conducted to confirm the acceptability of a product for its intended purpose. During the inspection process, the results for inspection characteristics are recorded and compared with predefined quality requirements. On the basis of this comparison, individual characteristics are accepted or rejected. At the conclusion of the inspection, on the

basis of inspection characteristic valuations, a usage decision is documented for the inspection lot. Typically, the entry of a usage decision for the inspection lot requires the documentation of inspection results for all required characteristics and processed optional characteristics, and the valuation of characteristics. In addition, the inspection lot must be released, the status of the inspection lot must permit the entry of the usage decision, the user must be authorized to execute the Usage Decision function and any required certificate must have been received. However, the usage decision for the inspection lot can be recorded irrespective of unevaluated inspection points. In this case, the user has two options. The inspection can be completed with the Usage Decision - Complete Inspection function. In this instance, the status of the inspection lot is changed to "close completed." As an alternative, the short-term characteristics can be closed by changing the status of the inspection lot to "short-term inspection completed" with the Usage Decision – Short-term Inspection function. In both cases, inspection results may not be revised unless the inspection lot status is reset.

Q-27.   A. Usage Decision - Overview of Stocks

A stock posting documents the entry or removal of a manufactured or procured material to or from stock. The stock posting ensures that the material in a stock-relevant inspection lot is properly accounted for, which contributes to effective logistics management and financial propriety. The Inspection Lot Completion component includes the functionality necessary to view stock in the inspection lot and then post the inspected materials to the appropriate stock account. The Usage Decision – Overview of Stocks is used for this purpose.

Q-28:   D. Material document

128

A stock posting documents the entry or removal of a manufactured or procured material to or from stock. The posting ensures that the material in a stock-relevant inspection lot is properly accounted for, which contributes to effective logistics management and financial propriety. The Inspection Lot Completion component includes the functionality necessary to display stock that has been posted to or from a particular inspection lot and to make additional stock postings. For example, as a usage decision for a material is recorded, the system automatically proposes a stock account to which the material can be posted. The stock account is proposed according to control indicators that are set for the usage decision codes. As stock is posted, a material document is created with reference to the inspection lot. Data in the material document includes the quantity of material in an inspection lot, the quantity of material posted with a usage decision and the quantity of material transferred from storage location A to storage location B.

Q-29:   C. Usage Decision

A stock posting documents the entry or removal of a manufactured or procured material to or from stock. The posting ensures that the material in a stock-relevant inspection lot is properly accounted for, which contributes to effective logistics management and financial propriety. The Inspection Lot Completion component includes the functionality necessary to display stock that has been posted to or from a particular inspection lot and to make additional stock postings. For example, as a usage decision for a material is recorded, the system automatically proposes a stock account to which the material can be posted. The stock account is proposed according to control indicators that are set for the usage decision codes.

Q-30:   A. Usage Decision

A quality inspection is conducted to confirm the acceptability of a product for its intended purpose. During the inspection process, the results for inspection characteristics are recorded and compared with predefined quality requirements. On the basis of this comparison, individual characteristics are accepted or rejected. At the conclusion of the inspection, on the basis of inspection characteristic valuations, a usage decision is documented for the inspection lot. As you document a usage decision for an inspection lot, it is possible to display characteristic inspection results that were documented as the inspection lot was processed. The summarized inspection results for an individual inspection lot can be accessed with the Usage Decision transaction. In turn, inspection results for several inspection lots can be displayed using an inspection characteristics evaluation function. In addition, a chronological history of characteristic inspection results can be accessed with the Results Recording and Usage Decision Results History function.

Q-31:   C. Usage Decision

A stock posting documents the entry or removal of a manufactured or procured material to or from stock. The posting ensures that the material in a stock-relevant inspection lot is properly accounted for, which contributes to effective logistics management and financial propriety. The Inspection Lot Completion component includes the functionality necessary to display stock that has been posted to or from a particular inspection lot and to make additional stock postings. The Usage Decision – Overview of Stocks is used for this purpose.

Q-32:   B. Usage Decision – Material Documents

A stock posting documents the entry or removal of a manufactured or procured material to or from stock.

The stock posting ensures that the material in a stock-relevant inspection lot is properly accounted for, which contributes to effective logistics management and financial propriety. The Inspection Lot Completion component usage decision function includes the functionality necessary to display stock that has been posted to or from a particular inspection lot and to make additional stock postings. For example, as a usage decision is recorded, the system can automatically propose a stock account to which the material in an inspection lot may be posted. The stock account is proposed according to control indicators that are set for usage decision codes, which are recorded at the conclusion of a quality inspection. The material documents that are created as stock was posted when an inspection lot is created can be displayed using the material documents list.

Q-33:   A. Create transfer posting from blocked stock to unrestricted use stock in Quality Management and C. Create return delivery for purchase order in Inventory Management

A stock posting documents the entry or removal of a manufactured or procured material to or from stock. The posting ensures that the material in a stock-relevant inspection lot is properly accounted for, which contributes to effective logistics management and financial propriety. The Inspection Lot Completion component includes the functionality necessary to display stock that has been posted to or from a particular inspection lot and to make additional stock postings. For example, as a usage decision for a material is recorded, the system automatically proposes a stock account to which the material can be posted. The stock account is proposed according to control indicators that are set for the usage decision codes. In the event that a stock posting was made in error, it can be reversed. To do so requires the original entry of a usage decision for an inspection lot, a stock posting for the transfer of stock from inspection stock to unrestricted use stock, the creation of a return delivery with reference to the original purchase order and the cancellation of the inspection lot.

Q-34:   A. Create list of defect records created for inspection lot, B. Identify defect types documented in defect records for an inspection lot and C. Activate notifications on the basis of the defect class of the defect code

A quality inspection is conducted to confirm the acceptability of a product for its intended purpose. During the inspection process, the results for inspection characteristics are recorded and compared with predefined quality requirements. On the basis of this comparison, individual characteristics are accepted or rejected. At the conclusion of the inspection, on the basis of inspection characteristic valuations, a usage decision is documented for the inspection lot. The system also provides four different overviews that are accessed by the Usage Decision function that support the Inspection Lot Completion transactions: Overview of Characteristics, Overview of Defects, Overview of Inspection Points and Overview of Stocks. In particular, the Overview of Defects displays information regarding the individual defects that impact a usage decision for an inspection lot. This overview displays the types of defects that were confirmed for an inspection lot and the defect structure, as well as provides a means to activate a quality notification.

Q-35:   A. Program executed with job management function

A quality inspection is conducted to confirm the acceptability of a product for its intended purpose.

During the inspection process, the results for inspection characteristics are recorded and compared with predefined quality requirements. On the basis of this comparison, individual characteristics are accepted or rejected. At the conclusion of the inspection, on the basis of inspection characteristic valuations, a usage decision is documented for the inspection lot. The usage decision can be recorded automatically by the system using a program, which is executed on a periodic basis with a job management function.

Q-36:   B. The four units can be posted to unrestricted use stock as a group and one object list can be assigned to the individual material document(s)

A stock posting documents the entry or removal of a manufactured or procured material to or from stock. The posting ensures that the material in a stock-relevant inspection lot is properly accounted for, which contributes to effective logistics management and financial propriety. The Inspection Lot Completion component includes the functionality necessary to display stock that has been posted to or from a particular inspection lot and to make additional stock postings. For example, as a usage decision for a material is recorded, the system automatically proposes a stock account to which the material can be posted. The stock account is proposed according to control indicators that are set for the usage decision codes. In the process, you can post one or more units of serialized material to a number of different stock accounts. An object list that documents each posting of serialized materials to a stock account is then created and assigned to each individual material document.

Q-37:   A. No inspection lot characteristic was rejected in the inspection lot and C. Defect records were created for critical defects and activated as notifications during the inspection

The acceptability of a product or material for its intended purpose is confirmed by a quality inspection. During an inspection, characteristic results are recorded and compared with predefined limits and valuation catalogs. On the basis of this comparison, individual characteristics are accepted or rejected. In turn, a usage decision is documented for the inspection lot on the basis of the valuation of individual inspection characteristics. The automatic entry of a usage decision for an inspection lot requires that inspection results be documented for all required characteristics and for processed optional characteristics. In addition, the inspection lot must be released, the status of the lot must permit the entry of the usage decision, any required certificate must be received, all characteristics must have been accepted in the lot, no defect records may have been created for the lot and an automatic usage decision must be planned for the material.

Q-38:   B. Usage decision code

A quality inspection is conducted to confirm the acceptability of a product for its intended purpose. During the inspection process, the results for inspection characteristics are recorded and compared with predefined quality requirements. On the basis of this comparison, individual characteristics are accepted or rejected. At the conclusion of the inspection, on the basis of inspection characteristic valuations, a usage decision is documented for the inspection lot. As the usage decision is documented, other functions are automatically performed by the system. For example, a quality score for the inspection lot is calculated and a quality level data record, which determines inspection stages for a subsequent inspection lot, is updated. Also, the Quality Management Information System is updated and follow-up actions are executed. In addition

to the automatic functions, the user may elect to perform other functions, as well. For example, the user can create defect records, create stock postings, confirm activities for quality orders and activate inactive quality notifications that were created to document a critical defect.

Q-39:   A. Enter the usage decision for the inspection lot

A quality inspection is conducted to confirm the acceptability of a product for its intended purpose. During the inspection process, the results for inspection characteristics are recorded and compared with predefined quality requirements. On the basis of this comparison, individual characteristics are accepted or rejected. At the conclusion of the inspection, on the basis of inspection characteristic valuations, a usage decision is documented for the inspection lot. In some circumstances, however, an authorized user may enter the usage decision for an inspection lot even if all required inspection points have not been valuated. In addition, the user might complete the valuation of the inspection points and then document a usage decision for the lot or discontinue the inspection.

Q-40:   C. Enter stock posting after the entry of a usage decision for an inspection lot

A quality inspection is conducted to confirm the acceptability of a product for its intended purpose. During the inspection process, the results for inspection characteristics are recorded and compared with predefined quality requirements. On the basis of this comparison, individual characteristics are accepted or rejected. At the conclusion of the inspection, on the basis of inspection characteristic valuations, a usage decision is documented for the inspection lot. As an alternative, the usage decisions for multiple inspection lots can be recorded simultaneously with the worklist function. This function requires that the user enter selection criteria, which the system uses to select inspection lots to be processed simultaneously. The system then displays the selected inspection lots in a worklist from which the user can select one or more lots and enter usage decisions for each of the selected lots simultaneously. After the usage decisions are posted for the inspection lots, the worklist function can also be used to post stock for multiple inspection lots.

Q-41:   B. Material is destroyed in an inspection

A stock posting documents the entry or removal of a manufactured or procured material to or from stock. The posting ensures that the material in a stock-relevant inspection lot is properly accounted for, which contributes to effective logistics management and financial propriety. The Inspection Lot Completion component includes the functionality necessary to display stock that has been posted to or from a particular inspection lot and to make additional stock postings. For example, as a usage decision for a material is recorded, the system automatically proposes a stock account to which the material can be posted. The stock account is proposed according to control indicators that are set for the usage decision codes. For example, material that is destroyed in an inspection can be posted to the sample usage stock account based on the control indicator that is set for the usage decision code, which is recorded at the conclusion of a quality inspection.

Q-42:   A. Sample usage and B. Return delivery

A stock posting documents the entry or removal of a manufactured or procured material to or from stock. The posting ensures that the material in a stock-relevant inspection lot is properly accounted for, which

contributes to effective logistics management and financial propriety. The Inspection Lot Completion component includes the functionality necessary to display stock that has been posted to or from a particular inspection lot and to make additional stock postings. For example, as a usage decision for a material is recorded, the system automatically proposes a stock account to which the material can be posted. The stock account is proposed according to control indicators that are set for the usage decision codes. For instance, material that is destroyed in an inspection can be posted to the sample usage stock account based on the control indicator that is set for usage decision code. Material can be posted from an inspection lot to the sample usage, return delivery, unrestricted use, scrap, blocked stock, reserves, and new material stock accounts.

Q-43: B. Control indicator in usage decision code

A stock posting documents the entry or removal of a manufactured or procured material to or from stock. The stock posting ensures that the material in a stock-relevant inspection lot is properly accounted for, which contributes to effective logistics management and financial propriety. The Inspection Lot Completion component includes the functionality necessary to make stock postings before, during or after a usage decision is recorded. For example, as a usage decision is recorded, the system can automatically propose a stock account to which the material in an inspection lot may be posted. For instance, material that is destroyed in an inspection can be posted to the sample usage stock account based on the control indicator that is set for usage decision code. Material can be posted from an inspection lot to the sample usage, return delivery, unrestricted use, scrap, blocked stock, reserves, and new material stock accounts.

Q-44:   B. Control indicator in usage decision code

A stock posting documents the entry or removal of a manufactured or procured material to or from stock. The posting ensures that the material in a stock-relevant inspection lot is properly accounted for, which contributes to effective logistics management and financial propriety. The Inspection Lot Completion component includes the functionality necessary to display stock that has been posted to or from a particular inspection lot and to make additional stock postings. For example, as a usage decision for a material is recorded, the system automatically proposes a stock account to which the material can be posted. The stock account is proposed according to control indicators that are set for the usage decision codes. For instance, material that is destroyed in an inspection can be posted to the sample usage stock account based on the control indicator that is set for usage decision code. Material can be posted from an inspection lot to the sample usage, return delivery, unrestricted use, scrap, blocked stock, reserves, and new material stock accounts.

Q-45:   C. Usage Decision

A stock posting documents the entry or removal of a manufactured or procured material to or from stock. The posting ensures that the material in a stock-relevant inspection lot is properly accounted for, which contributes to effective logistics management and financial propriety. The Inspection Lot Completion component includes the functionality necessary to display stock that has been posted to or from a particular inspection lot and to make additional stock postings. For example, as a usage decision for a material is recorded, the system automatically proposes a stock account to which the material can be posted. The stock account is proposed according to control indicators that are set for the usage decision codes. As the stock postings are made, the quantity of material destroyed during the inspection is calculated. The system then creates a proposal to post this quantity to the sample usage account. This function requires the activation of the destructive inspection control indicator for any inspection characteristic for which material is to be posted to the sample usage account. Stock postings for a destructive inspection can occur simultaneously with the automatic entry of the usage decision or the manual entry of the usage decision with automatic stock postings.

Q-46:   D. The "no change to batch status" control indicator was set in the set code

A stock posting documents the entry or removal of a manufactured or procured material to or from stock. The posting ensures that the material in a stock-relevant inspection lot is properly accounted for, which contributes to effective logistics management and financial propriety. In turn, the selection of a batch for shipment to a customer requires the selection of the stock proposal control indicator in catalog type 3 set code and the background processing control indicator in catalog type 3 set code.

Q-47:   B. Results Recording and C. Usage Decision

A quality inspection is conducted to confirm the acceptability of a product for its intended purpose. During the inspection process, the results for inspection characteristics are recorded and compared with predefined quality requirements. On the basis of this comparison, individual characteristics are accepted or rejected. At the conclusion of the inspection, on the basis of inspection characteristic valuations, a usage decision is documented for the inspection lot. This function, which is performed by the Results Recording and Usage Decision functions, each of which is integrated with the stock posting procedure.

Q-48:   D. Stock proposal control indicator in the usage decision code

A quality inspection is conducted to confirm the acceptability of a product for its intended purpose. During the inspection process, the results for inspection characteristics are recorded and compared with predefined quality requirements. On the basis of this comparison, individual characteristics are accepted or rejected. At the conclusion of the inspection, on the basis of inspection characteristic valuations, a usage decision is documented for the inspection lot. As the usage decision is documented, other functions are automatically performed by the system. For example, a quality score for the inspection lot is calculated and a quality level data record, which determines inspection stages for a subsequent inspection lot, is updated. Also, the Quality Management Information System is updated and follow-up actions are executed. In addition to the automatic functions, the user may elect to perform other functions, as well. For example, the user can create defect records, confirm activities for quality orders, activate inactive quality notifications that were created to document a critical defect and create stock postings. To determine the stock account to which material in an inspection lot is automatically posted, the stock proposal control indicator in the usage decision code is used.

Q-49:   B. Characteristic

A stock posting documents the entry or removal of a manufactured or procured material to or from stock. The posting ensures that the material in a stock-relevant inspection lot is properly accounted for, which

contributes to effective logistics management and financial propriety. The Inspection Lot Completion component includes the functionality necessary to display stock that has been posted to or from a particular inspection lot and to make additional stock postings. For example, as a usage decision for a material is recorded, the system automatically proposes a stock account to which the material can be posted. The stock account is proposed according to control indicators that are set for the usage decision codes. The control indicators for this posting are set in the characteristic.

Q-50:   A. Destructive inspection control indicator in the inspection characteristic

A stock posting documents the entry or removal of a manufactured or procured material to or from stock. The posting ensures that the material in a stock-relevant inspection lot is properly accounted for, which contributes to effective logistics management and financial propriety. The Inspection Lot Completion component includes the functionality necessary to display stock that has been posted to or from a particular inspection lot and to make additional stock postings. For example, as a usage decision for a material is recorded, the system automatically proposes a stock account to which the material can be posted. The stock account is proposed according to control indicators that are set for the usage decision codes. The stock proposal function requires the selection of the stock proposal control indicator in catalog type 3 set code and the background processing control indicator in catalog type 3 set code. The usage decision codes can be defined for a selected set that, in turn, is defined for an inspection type or for the inspection catalog type 3.

Q-51:   B. Batch status control indicator in the catalog type 3 code

141

A quality inspection is conducted to confirm the acceptability of a product for its intended purpose. During the inspection process, the results for inspection characteristics are recorded and compared with predefined quality requirements. On the basis of this comparison, individual characteristics are accepted or rejected. At the conclusion of the inspection, on the basis of inspection characteristic valuations, a usage decision is documented for the inspection lot. As the usage decision is documented, other functions are automatically performed by the system. For example, a quality score for the inspection lot is calculated and a quality level data record, which determines inspection stages for a subsequent inspection lot, is updated. Also, the Quality Management Information System is updated and follow-up actions are executed. In addition to the automatic functions, the user may elect to perform other functions, as well. For example, the user can create defect records, confirm activities for quality orders, activate quality notifications and create stock postings. The user can post stock-relevant material before, after or simultaneous to the entry of the usage decision. The account to which the stock is posted can be proposed by the system, on the basis of the Catalog type 3 usage decision code documented for the inspection lot. In addition, if the background processing control indicator is set in the usage decision set code, the stock is posted automatically to the appropriate account as the usage decision is recorded. In turn, the batch status control indicator in the usage decision code determines if the batch status is updated on the basis of the usage decision code and if so, if the status should be "restricted" or "unrestricted."

Q-52:   B. Usage Decision

A stock posting documents the entry or removal of a manufactured or procured material to or from stock. The stock posting ensures that the material in a stock-relevant inspection lot is properly accounted for, which contributes to effective logistics management and financial propriety. The Inspection Lot Completion component includes the functionality necessary to make stock postings before, during or after a usage decision is recorded. For example, as a usage decision is recorded, the system can automatically propose a stock account to which the material in an inspection lot can be posted. As stock is posted, a material document is created with reference to the inspection lot. A list of these documents, created with reference to an inspection lot, can be accessed with the Usage Decision – Material Documents function.

Q-53:   A. The documents in the list account for the original stock posting for the creation of a stock-relevant inspection lot and B. The documents in the list account for a decrease to the original stock in an inspection lot.

A stock posting documents the entry or removal of a manufactured or procured material to or from stock. The stock posting ensures that the material in a stock-relevant inspection lot is properly accounted for, which contributes to effective logistics management and financial propriety. The Inspection Lot Completion component includes the functionality necessary to make stock postings before, during or after a usage decision is recorded. For example, as a usage decision is recorded, the system can automatically propose a stock account to which the material in an inspection lot may be posted. As stock is posted, a material document is created with reference to the inspection lot. A list of material documents that are created with reference to an inspection lot can be accessed with the Usage Decision – Material Documents function.

Q-54:   A. Inspection Lot

A stock posting documents the entry or removal of a manufactured or procured material to or from stock. The stock posting ensures that the material in a stock-relevant inspection lot is properly accounted for, which contributes to effective logistics management and financial propriety. The Inspection Lot Completion component includes the functionality necessary to make stock postings before, during or after a usage decision is recorded. For example, as a usage decision is recorded, the system can automatically propose a stock account to which the material in an inspection lot may be posted. As stock is posted, a material document is created with reference to the inspection lot. A list of these documents, created with reference to an inspection lot, can be accessed with the Usage Decision – Material Documents function.

Q-55:   C. Usage Decision

A stock posting documents the entry or removal of a manufactured or procured material to or from stock. The stock posting ensures that the material in a stock-relevant inspection lot is properly accounted for, which contributes to effective logistics management and financial propriety. The Inspection Lot Completion component includes the functionality necessary to make stock postings before, during or after a usage decision is recorded. For example, as a usage decision is recorded, the system can automatically propose a stock account to which the material in an inspection lot may be posted. As stock is posted, a material document is created with reference to the inspection lot. A list of these documents, created with reference to an inspection lot, can be accessed with the Usage Decision – Material Documents function.

Q-56:   A. Display Material Documents for Inspection Lots and B. Record Defective Quantity

A quality inspection is conducted to confirm the acceptability of a product for its intended purpose. During the inspection process, the results for inspection characteristics are recorded and compared with predefined quality requirements. On the basis of this comparison, individual characteristics are accepted or rejected. At the conclusion of the inspection, on the basis of inspection characteristic valuations, a usage decision is documented for the inspection lot. As the usage decision is documented, other functions are automatically performed by the system. For example, a quality score for the inspection lot is calculated and a quality level data record, which determines inspection stages for a subsequent inspection lot, is updated. Also, the Quality Management Information System is updated and follow-up actions are executed. In addition to the automatic functions, the user may elect to perform other functions, as well. For example, the user can create defect records, create stock postings, confirm activities for quality orders and activate inactive quality notifications that were created to document a critical defect. A list of these documents, created with reference to an inspection lot, can be accessed with the Usage Decision – Material Documents function.

Q-57:   B. Stock account for stock destroyed in quality inspection

A stock posting documents the entry or removal of a manufactured or procured material to or from stock. The stock posting ensures that the material in a stock-relevant inspection lot is properly accounted for, which contributes to effective logistics management and

financial propriety. The Inspection Lot Completion component includes the functionality necessary to make stock postings before, during or after a usage decision is recorded. For example, as a usage decision is recorded, the system can automatically propose a stock account to which the material in an inspection lot may be posted. For instance, material that is destroyed in an inspection can be posted to the sample usage stock account based on the control indicator that is set for usage decision code. Material can be posted from an inspection lot to the sample usage, return delivery, unrestricted use, scrap, blocked stock, reserves, and new material stock accounts.

Q-58:   A. Destructive inspection for inspection characteristic control indicator and B. Stock proposal control indicator for usage decision set code

A stock posting documents the entry or removal of a manufactured or procured material to or from stock. The stock posting ensures that the material in a stock-relevant inspection lot is properly accounted for, which contributes to effective logistics management and financial propriety. The Inspection Lot Completion component includes the functionality necessary to make stock postings before, during or after a usage decision is recorded. For example, as a usage decision is recorded, the system can automatically propose a stock account to which the material in an inspection lot may be posted. In addition, as stock postings are made, the quantity of material destroyed during the inspection is calculated and posted to the sample usage account. This function requires the activation of the destructive inspection control indicator for any inspection characteristic for which material is to be posted to the sample usage account and the background processing control indicator for the usage decision set code. Stock postings for a destructive inspection can occur simultaneous with the manual or automatic entry of the usage decision.

Q-59: A. Stock proposal indicator for usage decision code and B. Background processing indicator for usage decision code

A quality inspection is conducted to confirm the acceptability of a product for its intended purpose. During the inspection process, the results for inspection characteristics are recorded and compared with predefined quality requirements. On the basis of this comparison, individual characteristics are accepted or rejected. At the conclusion of the inspection, on the basis of inspection characteristic valuations, a usage decision is documented for the inspection lot. As the usage decision is documented, other functions are automatically performed by the system. For example, a quality score for the inspection lot is calculated and a quality level data record, which determines inspection stages for a subsequent inspection lot, is updated. Also, the Quality Management Information System is updated and follow-up actions are executed. In addition to the automatic functions, the user may elect to perform other functions, as well. For example, the user can create defect records, confirm activities for quality orders, activate quality notifications and create stock postings. The user can post stock-relevant material before, after or simultaneous to the entry of the usage decision. The account to which the stock is posted can be proposed by the system, on the basis of the Catalog type 3 usage decision code documented for the inspection lot. In addition, if the background processing control indicator is set in the usage decision set code, the stock is posted automatically to the appropriate account as the usage decision is recorded. In turn, the batch status control indicator in the usage decision code determines if the batch status is updated on the basis of

the usage decision code and if so, if the status should be "restricted" or "unrestricted."

Q-60:   B. Stock proposal control indicator for usage decision set code and C. Background processing control indicator for usage decision code

A quality inspection is conducted to confirm the acceptability of a product for its intended purpose. During the inspection process, the results for inspection characteristics are recorded and compared with predefined quality requirements. On the basis of this comparison, individual characteristics are accepted or rejected. At the conclusion of the inspection, on the basis of inspection characteristic valuations, a usage decision is documented for the inspection lot. As the usage decision is documented, other functions are automatically performed by the system. For example, a quality score for the inspection lot is calculated and a quality level data record, which determines inspection stages for a subsequent inspection lot, is updated. Also, the Quality Management Information System is updated and follow-up actions are executed. In addition to the automatic functions, the user may elect to perform other functions, as well. For example, the user can create defect records, confirm activities for quality orders, activate quality notifications and create stock postings. The user can post stock-relevant material before, after or simultaneous to the entry of the usage decision. The account to which the stock is posted can be proposed by the system, on the basis of the Catalog type 3 usage decision code documented for the inspection lot. In addition, if the background processing control indicator is set in the usage decision set code, the stock is posted automatically to the appropriate account as the usage decision is recorded. In turn, the batch status control indicator in the usage decision code determines if the batch status is updated on the basis of

the usage decision code and if so, if the status should be "restricted" or "unrestricted."

Q-61:   B. Stock proposal control indicator for usage decision set code and C. Background processing control indicator for usage decision code

A quality inspection is conducted to confirm the acceptability of a product for its intended purpose. During the inspection process, the results for inspection characteristics are recorded and compared with predefined quality requirements. On the basis of this comparison, individual characteristics are accepted or rejected. At the conclusion of the inspection, on the basis of inspection characteristic valuations, a usage decision is documented for the inspection lot. As the usage decision is documented, other functions are automatically performed by the system. For example, a quality score for the inspection lot is calculated and a quality level data record, which determines inspection stages for a subsequent inspection lot, is updated. Also, the Quality Management Information System is updated and follow-up actions are executed. In addition to the automatic functions, the user may elect to perform other functions, as well. For example, the user can create defect records, confirm activities for quality orders, activate quality notifications and create stock postings. The user can post stock-relevant material before, after or simultaneous to the entry of the usage decision. The account to which the stock is posted can be proposed by the system, on the basis of the Catalog type 3 usage decision code documented for the inspection lot. In addition, if the background processing control indicator is set in the usage decision set code, the stock is posted automatically to the appropriate account as the usage decision is recorded. In turn, the batch status control indicator in the usage decision code determines if the batch status is updated on the basis of

the usage decision code and if so, if the status should be "restricted" or "unrestricted."

Q-62:   A. Usage Decision

A stock posting documents the entry or removal of a manufactured or procured material to or from stock. The stock posting ensures that the material in a stock-relevant inspection lot is properly accounted for, which contributes to effective logistics management and financial propriety. The Inspection Lot Completion component includes the functionality necessary to make stock postings before, during or after a usage decision is recorded. For example, as a usage decision is recorded, the system can automatically propose a stock account to which the material in an inspection lot may be posted. For instance, material that is destroyed in an inspection can be posted to the sample usage stock account based on the control indicator that is set for usage decision code. As stock is posted, a material document is created with reference to the inspection lot. A list of these documents, created with reference to an inspection lot, can be accessed with the Usage Decision – Material Documents function.

Q-63:   C. Background processing control indicator in usage decision set code

A quality inspection is conducted to confirm the acceptability of a product for its intended purpose. During the inspection process, the results for inspection characteristics are recorded and compared with predefined quality requirements. On the basis of this comparison, individual characteristics are accepted or rejected. At the conclusion of the inspection, on the basis of inspection characteristic valuations, a usage decision is documented for the inspection lot. The user can post stock-relevant material before, after or

150

simultaneous to the entry of the usage decision for the inspection lot. If the background processing control indicator is set in the usage decision set code, the stock is posted automatically to the appropriate account as the usage decision is recorded.

Q-64: D. Any of the above

A stock posting documents the entry or removal of a manufactured or procured material to or from stock. The stock posting ensures that the material in a stock-relevant inspection lot is properly accounted for, which contributes to effective logistics management and financial propriety. The Inspection Lot Completion component includes the functionality necessary to make stock postings before, during or after a usage decision is recorded. For example, as a usage decision is recorded, the system can automatically propose a stock account to which the material in an inspection lot may be posted. For instance, material that is destroyed in an inspection can be posted to the sample usage stock account based on the control indicator that is set for usage decision code. Material also can be posted from an inspection lot to the sample usage, return delivery, unrestricted use, scrap, blocked stock, reserves, and new material stock accounts.

Q-65: A. Release of the inspection lot and B. the authorization of the user to enter the usage decision for the inspection lot

A quality inspection is conducted to confirm the acceptability of a product for its intended purpose. During the inspection process, the results for inspection characteristics are recorded and compared with predefined quality requirements. On the basis of this comparison, individual characteristics are accepted or rejected. At the conclusion of the inspection, on the

basis of inspection characteristic valuations, a usage decision is documented for the inspection lot. The entry of the usage decision for the inspection lot requires the release of the inspection lot, the authorization of the user to enter the usage decision for the lot, the documentation of inspection results for all required characteristics and the receipt of any required certificate.

Q-66:   A. Stock posting before, during or after usage decision and C. Stock account to which material should be posted from an inspection lot

A stock posting documents the entry or removal of a manufactured or procured material to or from stock. The stock posting ensures that the material in a stock-relevant inspection lot is properly accounted for, which contributes to effective logistics management and financial propriety. The Inspection Lot Completion component includes the functionality necessary to make stock postings before, during or after a usage decision is recorded. For example, as a usage decision is recorded, the system can automatically propose a stock account to which the material in an inspection lot may be posted. For instance, material that is destroyed in an inspection can be posted to the sample usage stock account based on the control indicator that is set for usage decision code. Material can be posted from an inspection lot to the sample usage, return delivery, unrestricted use, scrap, blocked stock, reserves, and new material stock accounts.

Q-67:   B. Usage Decision

A quality inspection is conducted to confirm the acceptability of a product for its intended purpose. During the inspection process, the results for inspection characteristics are recorded and compared

with predefined quality requirements. On the basis of this comparison, individual characteristics are accepted or rejected. At the conclusion of the inspection, on the basis of inspection characteristic valuations, a usage decision is documented for the inspection lot. As the usage decision is documented, other functions are automatically performed by the system. For example, a quality score for the inspection lot is calculated and a quality level data record, which determines inspection stages for a subsequent inspection lot, is updated. Also, the Quality Management Information System is updated and follow-up actions are executed. In addition to the automatic functions, the user may elect to perform other functions, as well. For example, the user can confirm activities for quality orders, activate quality notifications, create stock postings and create and display defect records that were confirmed for the inspection lot with the Overview of Defects, which displays information regarding the individual defects that influence a usage decision for an inspection lot. This overview displays the types of defects that were confirmed for an inspection lot, the defect structure and provides a means to activate quality notifications.

Q-68:   A. Usage Decision - Overview of Defects

A quality inspection is conducted to confirm the acceptability of a product for its intended purpose. During the inspection process, the results for inspection characteristics are recorded and compared with predefined quality requirements. On the basis of this comparison, individual characteristics are accepted or rejected. At the conclusion of the inspection, on the basis of inspection characteristic valuations, a usage decision is documented for the inspection lot. As the usage decision is documented, other functions are automatically performed by the system. For example, a quality score for the inspection lot is calculated and a

153

quality level data record, which determines inspection stages for a subsequent inspection lot, is updated. Also, the Quality Management Information System is updated and follow-up actions are executed. In addition to the automatic functions, the user may elect to perform other functions, as well. For example, the user can confirm activities for quality orders, activate quality notifications, create stock postings and create and display defect records that were confirmed for the inspection lot with the Overview of Defects, which displays information regarding the individual defects that influence a usage decision for an inspection lot. This overview displays the types of defects that were confirmed for an inspection lot, the defect structure and provides a means to activate quality notifications.

Q-69:   A. Inspection results can be changed for an inspection lot unless the inspection is completed without a usage decision and B. Inspection results can be entered for the inspection lot after it is completed on a short-term basis

A quality inspection is conducted to confirm the acceptability of a product for its intended purpose. During the inspection process, the results for inspection characteristics are recorded and compared with predefined quality requirements. On the basis of this comparison, individual characteristics are accepted or rejected. At the conclusion of the inspection, on the basis of inspection characteristic valuations, a usage decision is documented for the inspection lot. Typically, the entry of the usage decision requires the closure of all required characteristics and processed optional characteristics. However, it may be necessary to complete an inspection even if inspection results have not been recorded for some required characteristics or some processed optional characteristics and if the usage decision is yet to be recorded. In this case, the user has two options. The inspection can be completed with the Usage Decision - Complete Inspection function. In this instance, the status of the inspection lot is changed to "close completed." As an alternative, the short-term characteristics can be closed by changing the status of the inspection lot to "short-term inspection completed" with the Usage Decision – Short-term Inspection function. In both cases, inspection results may be revised if the inspection lot status is reset.

Q-70:   B. Date of stock posting

A stock posting documents the entry or removal of a manufactured or procured material to or from stock. The stock posting ensures that the material in a stock-relevant inspection lot is properly accounted for, which contributes to effective logistics management and financial propriety. The Inspection Lot Completion component includes the functionality necessary to make stock postings before, during or after a usage decision is recorded. For example, as a usage decision is recorded, the system can automatically propose a stock account to which the material in a stock-relevant inspection lot may be posted. For instance, material that is destroyed in an inspection can be posted to the sample usage stock account based on the control indicator that is set for usage decision code. As stock is posted, a material document is created with reference to the inspection lot. Data in the material document includes the quantity of material in an inspection lot, the quantity of material posted with a usage decision and the quantity of material transferred from storage location A to storage location B. Also included are the reason for the stock posting, the date the material document is created, the date of the stock posting, text and possibly a cost center.

Q-71:   C. Usage Decision

A quality inspection is conducted to confirm the acceptability of a product for its intended purpose. During the inspection process, the results for inspection characteristics are recorded and compared with predefined quality requirements. On the basis of this comparison, individual characteristics are accepted or rejected. At the conclusion of the inspection, on the basis of inspection characteristic valuations, a usage decision is documented for the inspection lot. Typically, the entry of the usage decision requires the closure of all required characteristics and processed optional characteristics. However, it may be necessary to complete an inspection even if inspection results have not been recorded for some required characteristics or some processed optional characteristics and if the usage decision is yet to be recorded. In this case, the user has two options. The inspection can be completed with the Usage Decision - Complete Inspection function. In this instance, the status of the inspection lot is changed to "close completed." As an alternative, the short-term characteristics can be closed by changing the status of the inspection lot to "short-term inspection completed" with the Usage Decision – Short-term Inspection function. In both cases, inspection results may be revised if the inspection lot status is reset.

Q-72:   A. Material in inspection lot was posted to blocked stock

A stock posting documents the entry or removal of a manufactured or procured material to or from stock. The stock posting ensures that the material in a stock-relevant inspection lot is properly accounted for, which contributes to effective logistics management and financial propriety. The Inspection Lot Completion component includes the functionality necessary to make stock postings before, during or after a usage decision is recorded. For example, as a usage decision is recorded, the system can automatically propose a stock account to which the material in an inspection lot may be posted. For instance, material that is destroyed in an inspection can be posted to the sample usage stock account based on the control indicator that is set for usage decision code. As stock is posted, a material document is created with reference to the inspection lot. In the event that a stock posting was made in error, it can be reversed. To do so requires the original entry of a usage decision for an inspection lot, a stock posting for the transfer of stock from inspection stock to unrestricted use stock; the creation of a return delivery with reference to the original purchase order and the cancellation of the inspection lot.

Q-73:   E. None of the above

A stock posting documents the entry or removal of a manufactured or procured material to or from stock. The stock posting ensures that the material in a stock-relevant inspection lot is properly accounted for, which contributes to effective logistics management and financial propriety. The Inspection Lot Completion component includes the functionality necessary to make stock postings before, during or after a usage decision is recorded. For example, as a usage decision is recorded, the system can automatically propose a stock account to which the material in a stock-relevant inspection lot may be posted. For instance, material that is destroyed in an inspection can be posted to the sample usage stock account based on the control indicator that is set for usage decision code. As stock is posted, a material document is created with reference to the inspection lot.

Q-74:   B. Inspection lot number

A quality inspection is conducted to confirm the acceptability of a product for its intended purpose. During the inspection process, the results for inspection characteristics are recorded and compared with predefined quality requirements. On the basis of this comparison, individual characteristics are accepted or rejected. At the conclusion of the inspection, on the basis of inspection characteristic valuations, a usage decision is documented for the inspection lot. To record a usage decision, the user enters the inspection lot number and the usage decision code.

Q-75:   D. All of the above

A quality inspection is conducted to confirm the acceptability of a product for its intended purpose. During the inspection process, the results for inspection characteristics are recorded and compared with predefined quality requirements. On the basis of this comparison, individual characteristics are accepted or rejected. At the conclusion of the inspection, on the basis of inspection characteristic valuations, a usage decision is documented for the inspection lot. As the usage decision is documented, other functions are automatically performed by the system. For example, a quality score for the inspection lot is calculated and a quality level data record, which determines inspection stages for a subsequent inspection lot, is updated. Also, the Quality Management Information System is updated and follow-up actions are executed. In addition to the automatic functions, the user may elect to perform other functions, as well. For example, the user can confirm activities for quality orders, activate quality notifications, create stock postings and create and display defect records that were confirmed for the inspection lot with the Overview of Defects, which displays information regarding the individual defects that influence a usage decision for an inspection lot.

This overview displays the types of defects that were confirmed for an inspection lot, the defect structure and provides a means to activate quality notifications.

Q-76:   B. Complete Inspection on Short-term Basis and D. Create Usage Decision

A quality inspection is conducted to confirm the acceptability of a product for its intended purpose. During the inspection process, the results for inspection characteristics are recorded and compared with predefined quality requirements. On the basis of this comparison, individual characteristics are accepted or rejected. At the conclusion of the inspection, on the basis of inspection characteristic valuations, a usage decision is documented for the inspection lot with the Create Usage Decision function. Typically, the entry of the usage decision requires the closure of all required characteristics and processed optional characteristics. However, it may be necessary to complete an inspection even if inspection results have not been recorded for some required characteristics or some processed optional characteristics and if the usage decision is yet to be recorded. In this case, the user has two options. The inspection can be completed with the Usage Decision - Complete Inspection function. In this instance, the status of the inspection lot is changed to "close completed." As an alternative, the short-term characteristics can be closed by changing the status of the inspection lot to "short-term inspection completed" with the Usage Decision – Short-term Inspection function.

Q-77:   A. Reverse Stock Posting

A quality inspection is conducted to confirm the acceptability of a product for its intended purpose. During the inspection process, the results for inspection characteristics are recorded and compared

with predefined quality requirements. On the basis of this comparison, individual characteristics are accepted or rejected. At the conclusion of the inspection, on the basis of inspection characteristic valuations, a usage decision is documented for the inspection lot. As the usage decision is documented, other functions are automatically performed by the system. For example, a quality score for the inspection lot is calculated and a quality level data record, which determines inspection stages for a subsequent inspection lot, is updated. Also, the Quality Management Information System is updated and follow-up actions are executed. In addition to the automatic functions, the user may elect to perform other functions, as well. For example, the user can confirm activities for quality orders, activate quality notifications, create and reverse stock postings and create and display defect records that were confirmed for the inspection lot.

Q-78:   A. Confirm the receipt of a certificate and C. Display defect structure

A quality inspection is conducted to confirm the acceptability of a product for its intended purpose. During the inspection process, the results for inspection characteristics are recorded and compared with predefined quality requirements. On the basis of this comparison, individual characteristics are accepted or rejected. At the conclusion of the inspection, on the basis of inspection characteristic valuations, a usage decision is documented for the inspection lot. As the usage decision is documented, other functions are automatically performed by the system. For example, a quality score for the inspection lot is calculated and a quality level data record, which determines inspection stages for a subsequent inspection lot, is updated. Also, the Quality Management Information System is updated and follow-up actions are executed. In addition to the automatic functions, the user may elect to perform other functions, as well. For example, the user can create defect records, confirm activities for quality orders, confirm the receipt of a certificate, activate quality notifications, create stock postings and record the number of defective units in the inspection lot.

Q-79:   A. Determine the types of defects confirmed for an inspection lot and C. Determine the hierarchical level at which defect records were created

A quality inspection is conducted to confirm the acceptability of a product for its intended purpose. During the inspection process, the results for inspection characteristics are recorded and compared with predefined quality requirements. On the basis of this comparison, individual characteristics are accepted or rejected. At the conclusion of the inspection, on the basis of inspection characteristic valuations, a usage decision is documented for the inspection lot. As the usage decision is documented, other functions are automatically performed by the system. For example, a quality score for the inspection lot is calculated and a quality level data record, which determines inspection stages for a subsequent inspection lot, is updated. Also, the Quality Management Information System is updated and follow-up actions are executed. In addition to the automatic functions, the user may elect to perform other functions, as well. For example, the user can confirm activities for quality orders, activate quality notifications, create stock postings and create and display defect records that were confirmed for the inspection lot with the Overview of Defects, which displays information regarding the individual defects that influence a usage decision for an inspection lot. This overview displays the types of defects that were confirmed for an inspection lot and the defect structure.

Q-80:   B. Share of defects in inspection lot and C. Share of defects for characteristics

A quality inspection is conducted to confirm the acceptability of a product for its intended purpose. During the inspection process, the results for inspection characteristics are recorded and compared with predefined quality requirements. On the basis of this comparison, individual characteristics are accepted or rejected. At the conclusion of the inspection, on the basis of inspection characteristic valuations, a usage decision is documented for the inspection lot. As the usage decision is documented, other functions are automatically performed by the system. For example, a quality score for the inspection lot is calculated on the basis of the share of defects in the inspection lot or the share of defects for characteristics and a quality level data record, which determines inspection stages for a subsequent inspection lot, is updated. Also, the Quality Management Information System is updated and follow-up actions are executed. In addition to the automatic functions, the user may elect to perform other functions, as well. For example, the user can confirm activities for quality orders, activate quality notifications, create stock postings and create and display defect records that were confirmed for the inspection lot.

Q-81:   D. Usage decision for the inspection lot

A quality inspection is conducted to confirm the acceptability of a product for its intended purpose. During the inspection process, the results for inspection characteristics are recorded and compared with predefined quality requirements. On the basis of this comparison, individual characteristics are accepted or rejected. At the conclusion of the inspection, on the basis of inspection characteristic valuations, a usage decision is documented for the inspection lot. As the

usage decision is documented, other functions are automatically performed by the system. For example, a quality score for the inspection lot is calculated on the basis of the share of defects in the inspection lot or the share of defects for characteristics and a quality level data record, which determines inspection stages for a subsequent inspection lot, is updated. Also, the Quality Management Information System is updated and follow-up actions are executed. In addition to the automatic functions, the user may elect to perform other functions, as well. For example, the user can confirm activities for quality orders, activate quality notifications, create stock postings and create and display defect records that were confirmed for the inspection lot.

Q-82:   A. Calculate quality score for the inspection lot, C. Trigger follow-up actions and D. Update quality level

A quality inspection is conducted to confirm the acceptability of a product for its intended purpose. During the inspection process, the results for inspection characteristics are recorded and compared with predefined quality requirements. On the basis of this comparison, individual characteristics are accepted or rejected. At the conclusion of the inspection, on the basis of inspection characteristic valuations, a usage decision is documented for the inspection lot. As the usage decision is documented, other functions are automatically performed by the system. For example, a quality score for the inspection lot is calculated on the basis of the share of defects in the inspection lot or the share of defects for characteristics and a quality level data record, which determines inspection stages for a subsequent inspection lot, is updated. Also, the Quality Management Information System is updated and follow-up actions are executed. In addition to the automatic functions, the user may elect to perform other functions, as well. For example, the user can confirm activities for quality orders, activate quality notifications, create stock postings and create and display defect records that were confirmed for the inspection lot.

Q-83:   A. Batches, C. Catalogs and E. Inspection Lot Creation

A quality inspection is conducted to confirm the acceptability of a product for its intended purpose. During the inspection process, the results for inspection characteristics are recorded and compared with predefined quality requirements. On the basis of this comparison, individual characteristics are accepted or rejected. At the conclusion of the inspection, on the basis of inspection characteristic valuations, a usage decision is documented for the inspection lot. As the usage decision is documented, other functions are automatically performed by the system. For example, a quality score for the inspection lot is calculated and a quality level data record, which determines inspection stages for a subsequent inspection lot, is updated. Also, the Quality Management Information System is updated and follow-up actions are executed. These functions require the implementation of other components in addition to the Inspection Lot Completion component, such as the Catalog, Materials Management and Production Planning components. Also needed are the Sales and Distribution, Plant Maintenance and Batches components.

Q-84:   A. Usage Decision - Defect Structure

A quality inspection is conducted to confirm the acceptability of a product for its intended purpose. During the inspection process, the results for inspection characteristics are recorded and compared with predefined quality requirements. On the basis of

this comparison, individual characteristics are accepted or rejected. At the conclusion of the inspection, on the basis of inspection characteristic valuations, a usage decision is documented for the inspection lot. As the usage decision is documented, other functions are automatically performed by the system. For example, a quality score for the inspection lot is calculated on the basis of the share of defects in the inspection lot or the share of defects for characteristics and a quality level data record, which determines inspection stages for a subsequent inspection lot, is updated. Also, the Quality Management Information System is updated and follow-up actions are executed. In addition to the automatic functions, the user may elect to perform other functions, as well. For example, the user can confirm activities for quality orders, activate quality notifications, create stock postings and create and display defect records that were confirmed for the inspection lot.

Q-85:   A. Usage decision code

A quality inspection is conducted to confirm the acceptability of a product for its intended purpose. During the inspection process, the results for inspection characteristics are recorded and compared with predefined quality requirements. On the basis of this comparison, individual characteristics are accepted or rejected. At the conclusion of the inspection, on the basis of inspection characteristic valuations, a usage decision is documented for the inspection lot. As the usage decision is documented, on the basis of the usage decision code, other functions are automatically performed by the system. For example, a quality score for the inspection lot is calculated on the basis of the share of defects in the inspection lot or the share of defects for characteristics and a quality level data record, which determines inspection stages for a subsequent inspection lot, is updated. Also, the Quality

Management Information System is updated and follow-up actions are executed. In addition to the automatic functions, the user may elect to perform other functions, as well. For example, the user can confirm activities for quality orders, activate quality notifications, create stock postings and create and display defect records that were confirmed for the inspection lot.

Q-86:   B. Display defect structure

A quality inspection is conducted to confirm the acceptability of a product for its intended purpose. During the inspection process, the results for inspection characteristics are recorded and compared with predefined quality requirements. On the basis of this comparison, individual characteristics are accepted or rejected. At the conclusion of the inspection, on the basis of inspection characteristic valuations, a usage decision is documented for the inspection lot. As the usage decision is documented, other functions are automatically performed by the system. For example, a quality score for the inspection lot is calculated and a quality level data record, which determines inspection stages for a subsequent inspection lot, is updated. Also, the Quality Management Information System is updated and follow-up actions are executed. In addition to the automatic functions, the user may elect to perform other functions, as well. For example, the user can confirm activities for quality orders, activate quality notifications, create stock postings and create and display defect records that were confirmed for the inspection lot with the Overview of Defects, which displays information regarding the individual defects that influence a usage decision for an inspection lot. This overview displays the types of defects that were confirmed for an inspection lot and the defect structure.

Q-87:   C. Usage Decision

A quality inspection is conducted to confirm the acceptability of a product for its intended purpose. During the inspection process, the results for inspection characteristics are recorded and compared with predefined quality requirements. On the basis of this comparison, individual characteristics are accepted or rejected. At the conclusion of the inspection, on the basis of inspection characteristic valuations, a usage decision is documented for the inspection lot. As the usage decision is documented, other functions are automatically performed by the system. For example, a quality score for the inspection lot is calculated and a quality level data record, which determines inspection stages for a subsequent inspection lot, is updated. Also, the Quality Management Information System is updated and follow-up actions are executed. In addition to the automatic functions, the user may elect to perform other functions, as well. For example, the user can confirm activities for quality orders, activate quality notifications, create stock postings and create and display defect records that were confirmed for the inspection lot.

Q-88:   A. Inspection type

A quality inspection is conducted to confirm the acceptability of a product for its intended purpose. During the inspection process, the results for inspection characteristics are recorded and compared with predefined quality requirements. On the basis of this comparison, individual characteristics are accepted or rejected. At the conclusion of the inspection, on the basis of inspection characteristic valuations, a usage decision is documented for the inspection lot. As the usage decision is documented, other functions are automatically performed by the system. For example, a

quality score for the inspection lot is calculated based on the usage decision code and inspection type, and a quality level data record, which determines inspection stages for a subsequent inspection lot, is updated. Also, the Quality Management Information System is updated and follow-up actions are executed. In addition to the automatic functions, the user may elect to perform other functions, as well. For example, the user can confirm activities for quality orders, activate quality notifications, create stock postings and create and display defect records that were confirmed for the inspection lot.

Q-89:   B. Results Recording and C. Usage Decision

A quality inspection is conducted to confirm the acceptability of a product for its intended purpose. During the inspection process, the results for inspection characteristics are recorded and compared with predefined quality requirements. On the basis of this comparison, individual characteristics are accepted or rejected. At the conclusion of the inspection, on the basis of inspection characteristic valuations, a usage decision is documented for the inspection lot. As the usage decision is documented, other functions are automatically performed by the system. For example, a quality score for the inspection lot is calculated and a quality level data record, which determines inspection stages for a subsequent inspection lot, is updated. Also, the Quality Management Information System is updated and follow-up actions are executed. In addition to the automatic functions, the user may elect to perform other functions, as well. For example, as the usage decision is documented, it's possible to display characteristic inspection results that were documented as the inspection lot was processed. The summarized inspection results for an individual inspection lot can be viewed with the Usage Decision transaction. In turn, inspection results for several inspection lots can be displayed using an inspection characteristics evaluation function. In addition, a chronological history of characteristic inspection results can be viewed with the Results Recording and Usage Decision Results History function.

Q-90:   A. Activate quality notification, D. Create stock posting and E. Confirm activities for inspection operation

A quality inspection is conducted to confirm the acceptability of a product for its intended purpose. During the inspection process, the results for inspection characteristics are recorded and compared with predefined quality requirements. On the basis of this comparison, individual characteristics are accepted or rejected. At the conclusion of the inspection, on the basis of inspection characteristic valuations, a usage decision is documented for the inspection lot. As the usage decision is documented, other functions are automatically performed by the system. For example, a quality score for the inspection lot is calculated and a quality level data record, which determines inspection stages for a subsequent inspection lot, is updated. Also, the Quality Management Information System is updated and follow-up actions are executed. In addition to the automatic functions, the user may elect to perform other functions, as well. For example, the user can create defect records, confirm activities for quality orders, activate quality notifications, create stock postings, and record the number of defective units in the inspection lot.

Q-91:   C. Usage Decision

A quality inspection is conducted to confirm the acceptability of a product for its intended purpose.

During the inspection process, the results for inspection characteristics are recorded and compared with predefined quality requirements. On the basis of this comparison, individual characteristics are accepted or rejected. At the conclusion of the inspection, on the basis of inspection characteristic valuations, a usage decision is documented for the inspection lot. As the usage decision is documented, other functions are automatically performed by the system. For example, a quality score for the inspection lot is calculated based on the usage decision code and inspection type, and a quality level data record, which determines inspection stages for a subsequent inspection lot, is updated. Also, the Quality Management Information System is updated and follow-up actions are executed. In addition to the automatic functions, the user may elect to perform other functions, as well. For example, the user can confirm activities for quality orders, activate quality notifications, create stock postings and create and display defect records that were confirmed for the inspection lot.

Q-92:   A. Create defect record and C. Confirm activities for inspection operation

A quality inspection is conducted to confirm the acceptability of a product for its intended purpose. During the inspection process, the results for inspection characteristics are recorded and compared with predefined quality requirements. On the basis of this comparison, individual characteristics are accepted or rejected. At the conclusion of the inspection, on the basis of inspection characteristic valuations, a usage decision is documented for the inspection lot. As the usage decision is documented, other functions are automatically performed by the system. For example, a quality score for the inspection lot is calculated based on the usage decision code and inspection type, and a quality level data record, which determines inspection stages for a subsequent inspection lot, is updated. Also, the Quality Management Information System is updated and follow-up actions are executed. In addition to the automatic functions, the user may elect to perform other functions, as well. For example, the user can confirm activities for quality orders, activate quality notifications, create stock postings and create and display defect records that were confirmed for the inspection lot.

Q-93:   A. Recorded results cannot be changed subsequent to the documentation of a usage decision

A quality inspection is conducted to confirm the acceptability of a product for its intended purpose. During the inspection process, the results for inspection characteristics are recorded and compared with predefined quality requirements. On the basis of this comparison, individual characteristics are accepted or rejected. At the conclusion of the inspection, on the basis of inspection characteristic valuations, a usage decision is documented for the inspection lot. After an inspection lot is completed, the lot's inspection results can't be changed unless the status of the lot is reset.

Q-94:   A. Recorded results for required inspection characteristics

A quality inspection is conducted to confirm the acceptability of a product for its intended purpose. During the inspection process, the results for inspection characteristics are recorded and compared with predefined quality requirements. On the basis of this comparison, individual characteristics are accepted or rejected. At the conclusion of the inspection, on the basis of the valuation of required individual inspection characteristics, a usage decision is documented for the inspection lot.

Q-95:   B. Results recorded for required inspection characteristics and C. Authorization to record usage decision

A quality inspection is conducted to confirm the acceptability of a product for its intended purpose. During the inspection process, the results for inspection characteristics are recorded and compared with predefined quality requirements. On the basis of this comparison, individual characteristics are accepted or rejected. At the conclusion of the inspection, on the basis of inspection characteristic valuations, a usage decision is documented for the inspection lot. The entry of a usage decision for an inspection lot requires the closure of all required characteristics and processed optional characteristics. In addition, the inspection lot must be released, the status of the inspection lot must permit the entry of the usage decision, the user must have the authorization to execute the Usage Decision function, and any required certificate must have been received.

Q-96:   B. Inspection type

A quality inspection is conducted to confirm the acceptability of a product for its intended purpose. During the inspection process, the results for inspection characteristics are recorded and compared with predefined quality requirements. On the basis of this comparison, individual characteristics are accepted or rejected. At the conclusion of the inspection, on the basis of inspection characteristic valuations, a usage decision is documented for the inspection lot. As the usage decision is documented, other functions are automatically performed by the system. For example, a quality score for the inspection lot is calculated based on the usage decision code and inspection type, and a quality level data record, which determines inspection

172

stages for a subsequent inspection lot, is updated. Also, the Quality Management Information System is updated and follow-up actions are executed. In addition to the automatic functions, the user may elect to perform other functions, as well. For example, the user can confirm activities for quality orders, activate quality notifications, create stock postings and create and display defect records that were confirmed for the inspection lot.

Q-97:   A. Sample size and B. Acceptance number

A quality inspection is conducted to confirm the acceptability of a product for its intended purpose. During the inspection process, the results for inspection characteristics are recorded and compared with predefined quality requirements, such as sample size and acceptance number. On the basis of this comparison, individual characteristics are accepted or rejected. At the conclusion of the inspection, on the basis of inspection characteristic valuations, a usage decision is documented for the inspection lot. As the usage decision is documented, other functions are automatically performed by the system. For example, a quality score for the inspection lot is calculated and a quality level data record, which determines inspection stages for a subsequent inspection lot, is updated. Also, the Quality Management Information System is updated and follow-up actions are executed. In addition to the automatic functions, the user may elect to perform other functions, as well. For example, the user can create defect records, confirm activities for quality orders, activate quality notifications, create stock postings, and record the number of defective units in the inspection lot.

Q-98:   A. Required characteristics must be closed prior to entry of the usage decision

A quality inspection is conducted to confirm the acceptability of a product for its intended purpose. During the inspection process, the results for inspection characteristics are recorded and compared with predefined quality requirements. On the basis of this comparison, individual characteristics are accepted or rejected. At the conclusion of the inspection, on the basis of inspection characteristic valuations, a usage decision is documented for the inspection lot. The entry of this usage decision typically requires the closure of all required characteristics and processed optional characteristics. In addition, the inspection lot must be released, the status of the inspection lot must permit the entry of the usage decision, the user must have the authorization to execute the Usage Decision function, and any required certificate must have been received.

Q-99:   A. Create stock posting

A stock posting documents the entry or removal of a manufactured or procured material to or from stock. The stock posting ensures that the material in a stock-relevant inspection lot is properly accounted for, which contributes to effective logistics management and financial propriety. The Inspection Lot Completion component includes the functionality necessary to view stock in the inspection lot and then post the inspected materials to the appropriate stock account. The Usage Decision – Overview of Stocks is used for this purpose.

Q-100:   D. Overview of Stocks

A stock posting documents the entry or removal of a manufactured or procured material to or from stock. The stock posting ensures that the material in a stock-relevant inspection lot is properly accounted for, which contributes to effective logistics management and

financial propriety. The Inspection Lot Completion component includes the functionality necessary to make stock postings before, during or after a usage decision is recorded. For example, as a usage decision is recorded, the system can automatically propose a stock account to which the material in an inspection lot may be posted. For instance, material that is destroyed in an inspection can be posted to the sample usage stock account based on the control indicator that is set for usage decision code. As stock is posted, a material document is created with reference to the inspection lot. The Inspection Lot Completion component includes the functionality necessary to view stock in the inspection lot and then post the inspected materials to the appropriate stock account. The Usage Decision – Overview of Stocks is used for this purpose.

Q-101:   A. Usage Decision - Overview of Characteristics

A quality inspection is conducted to confirm the acceptability of a product for its intended purpose. During the inspection process, the results for inspection characteristics are recorded and compared with predefined quality requirements. On the basis of this comparison, individual characteristics are accepted or rejected. At the conclusion of the inspection, on the basis of inspection characteristic valuations, a usage decision is documented for the inspection lot. As the usage decision is documented, other functions are automatically performed by the system. For example, a quality score for the inspection lot is calculated and a quality level data record, which determines inspection stages for a subsequent inspection lot, is updated. Also, the Quality Management Information System is updated and follow-up actions are executed. In addition to the automatic functions, the user may elect to perform other functions, as well. For example, the user can confirm activities for quality orders, activate quality notifications, create stock postings and create and display defect records that were confirmed for the inspection lot. To support inspection lot completion functions, the system provides four different overviews that are accessed by the Usage Decision function: Overview of Characteristics, Overview of Defects, Overview of Inspection Points and Overview of Stocks. In particular, the Overview of Characteristics displays the status and valuation of characteristics in an inspection lot.

Q-102: A. Overview of Characteristics, B. Overview of Defects and C. Overview of Stocks

A quality inspection is conducted to confirm the acceptability of a product for its intended purpose. During the inspection process, the results for inspection characteristics are recorded and compared with predefined quality requirements. On the basis of this comparison, individual characteristics are accepted or rejected. At the conclusion of the inspection, on the basis of inspection characteristic valuations, a usage decision is documented for the inspection lot. As the usage decision is documented, other functions are automatically performed by the system. For example, a quality score for the inspection lot is calculated and a quality level data record, which determines inspection stages for a subsequent inspection lot, is updated. Also, the Quality Management Information System is updated and follow-up actions are executed. In addition to the automatic functions, the user may elect to perform other functions, as well. For example, the user can confirm activities for quality orders, activate quality notifications, create stock postings and create and display defect records that were confirmed for the inspection lot. To support inspection lot completion functions, the system provides four different overviews that are accessed by the Usage Decision function: Overview of Characteristics, Overview of Defects, Overview of Inspection Points and Overview of Stocks.

Q-103: A. True

A quality inspection is conducted to confirm the acceptability of a product for its intended purpose. During the inspection process, the results for inspection characteristics are recorded and compared with predefined quality requirements. On the basis of this comparison, individual characteristics are accepted or rejected. At the conclusion of the inspection, on the basis of inspection characteristic valuations, a usage decision is documented for the inspection lot. As the usage decision is documented, other functions are automatically performed by the system. For example, a quality score for the inspection lot is calculated and a quality level data record, which determines inspection stages for a subsequent inspection lot, is updated. Also, the Quality Management Information System is updated and follow-up actions are executed. In addition to the automatic functions, the user may elect to perform other functions, as well. For example, the user can confirm activities for quality orders, activate quality notifications, create stock postings and create and display defect records that were confirmed for the inspection lot. Both defect records and notifications can be created before or after the entry of a usage decision.

Q-104: C. Usage Decision - Overview of Defects

A quality inspection is conducted to confirm the acceptability of a product for its intended purpose. During the inspection process, the results for inspection characteristics are recorded and compared

with predefined quality requirements. On the basis of this comparison, individual characteristics are accepted or rejected. At the conclusion of the inspection, on the basis of inspection characteristic valuations, a usage decision is documented for the inspection lot. As the usage decision is documented, other functions are automatically performed by the system. For example, a quality score for the inspection lot is calculated and a quality level data record, which determines inspection stages for a subsequent inspection lot, is updated. Also, the Quality Management Information System is updated and follow-up actions are executed. In addition to the automatic functions, the user may elect to perform other functions, as well. For example, the user can confirm activities for quality orders, activate quality notifications, create stock postings and create and display defect records that were confirmed for the inspection lot with the Overview of Defects, which displays information regarding the individual defects that influence a usage decision for an inspection lot. This overview displays the types of defects that were confirmed for an inspection lot and the defect structure.

Q-105:   A. Overview of Stocks and C. Overview of Defects

A quality inspection is conducted to confirm the acceptability of a product for its intended purpose. During the inspection process, the results for inspection characteristics are recorded and compared with predefined quality requirements. On the basis of this comparison, individual characteristics are accepted or rejected. At the conclusion of the inspection, on the basis of inspection characteristic valuations, a usage decision is documented for the inspection lot. As the usage decision is documented, other functions are automatically performed by the system. For example, a

quality score for the inspection lot is calculated and a quality level data record, which determines inspection stages for a subsequent inspection lot, is updated. Also, the Quality Management Information System is updated and follow-up actions are executed. In addition to the automatic functions, the user may elect to perform other functions, as well. For example, the user can confirm activities for quality orders, activate quality notifications, create stock postings and create and display defect records. In addition to the functionality required to record a usage decision at the conclusion of a quality inspection, the Inspection Lot Completion component also provides four different overviews that support the completion of the inspection lot: Overview of Characteristics, Overview of Defects, Overview of Inspection Points and Overview of Stocks.

Q-106:   A. Usage Decision - Overview of Defects

A quality inspection is conducted to confirm the acceptability of a product for its intended purpose. During the inspection process, the results for inspection characteristics are recorded and compared with predefined quality requirements. On the basis of this comparison, individual characteristics are accepted or rejected. At the conclusion of the inspection, on the basis of inspection characteristic valuations, a usage decision is documented for the inspection lot. As the usage decision is documented, other functions are automatically performed by the system. For example, a quality score for the inspection lot is calculated and a quality level data record, which determines inspection stages for a subsequent inspection lot, is updated. Also, the Quality Management Information System is updated and follow-up actions are executed. In addition to the automatic functions, the user may elect to perform other functions, as well. For example, the user can confirm activities for quality orders, activate quality notifications, create stock postings and create and display defect records that were confirmed for the inspection lot with the Overview of Defects, which displays information regarding the individual defects that influence a usage decision for an inspection lot. This overview displays the types of defects that were confirmed for an inspection lot and the defect structure.

Q-107:   B. Usage Decision

A quality inspection is conducted to confirm the acceptability of a product for its intended purpose. During the inspection process, the results for inspection characteristics are recorded and compared with predefined quality requirements. On the basis of this comparison, individual characteristics are accepted or rejected. At the conclusion of the inspection, on the basis of inspection characteristic valuations, a usage decision is documented for the inspection lot. As the usage decision is documented, other functions are automatically performed by the system. For example, a quality score for the inspection lot is calculated and a quality level data record, which determines inspection stages for a subsequent inspection lot, is updated. Also, the Quality Management Information System is updated and follow-up actions are executed. In addition to the automatic functions, the user may elect to perform other functions, as well. For example, the user can confirm activities for quality orders, activate quality notifications, create stock postings and create and display defect records that were confirmed for the inspection lot with the Overview of Defects, which displays information regarding the individual defects that influence a usage decision for an inspection lot. This overview displays the types of defects that were confirmed for an inspection lot and the defect structure.

Q-108:   D. Post a quantity of material to a particular stock type

A stock posting documents the entry or removal of a manufactured or procured material to or from stock. The stock posting ensures that the material in a stock-relevant inspection lot is properly accounted for, which contributes to effective logistics management and financial propriety. The Inspection Lot Completion component includes the functionality necessary to make stock postings before, during or after a usage decision is recorded. For example, as a usage decision is recorded, the system can automatically propose a stock account to which the material in an inspection lot may be posted. For instance, material that is destroyed in an inspection can be posted to the sample usage stock account based on the control indicator that is set for usage decision code. As stock is posted, a material document is created with reference to the inspection lot. The Inspection Lot Completion component includes the functionality necessary to view stock in the inspection lot and then post the inspected materials to the appropriate stock account. The Usage Decision – Overview of Stocks is used for this purpose.

Q-109:   A. Reset status of the inspection lot

A quality inspection is conducted to confirm the acceptability of a product for its intended purpose. During the inspection process, the results for inspection characteristics are recorded and compared with predefined quality requirements. On the basis of this comparison, individual characteristics are accepted or rejected. At the conclusion of the inspection, on the basis of inspection characteristic valuations, a usage decision is documented for the inspection lot. The entry of the usage decision typically requires the closure of all required characteristics and processed optional characteristics. However, it may be necessary to complete an inspection even if all inspection results have not been recorded for some required characteristics or some processed optional characteristics. In this case, the user has two options. The inspection can be completed with the Usage Decision - Complete Inspection function. In this instance, the status of the inspection lot is changed to "close completed." As an alternative, the short-term characteristics can be closed by changing the status of the inspection lot to "short-term inspection completed" with the Usage Decision – Short-term Inspection function. In both cases, inspection results may not be revised unless the inspection lot status is reset.

Q-110:   C. Discontinue the inspection

A quality inspection is conducted to confirm the acceptability of a product for its intended purpose. During the inspection process, the results for inspection characteristics are recorded and compared with predefined quality requirements. On the basis of this comparison, individual characteristics are accepted or rejected. At the conclusion of the inspection, on the basis of inspection characteristic valuations, a usage decision is documented for the inspection lot. Typically, the entry of a usage decision for the inspection lot requires the documentation of inspection results for all required characteristics and processed optional characteristics, and the valuation of characteristics. In addition, the inspection lot must be released, the status of the inspection lot must permit the entry of the usage decision, the user must be authorized to execute the Usage Decision function and any required certificate must have been received. Even if all inspection points have not been valuated, the usage decision for the inspection lot can be recorded, the inspection can be discontinued or the remaining inspection points can be valuated and a usage decision recorded.

Q-111: C. Authorization to make usage decision

A quality inspection is conducted to confirm the acceptability of a product for its intended purpose. During the inspection process, the results for inspection characteristics are recorded and compared with predefined quality requirements. On the basis of this comparison, individual characteristics are accepted or rejected. At the conclusion of the inspection, on the basis of inspection characteristic valuations, a usage decision is documented for the inspection lot. The entry of a usage decision for the inspection lot requires that inspection results have been documented for all required characteristics and for processed optional characteristics. In addition, the inspection lot must be released, the status of the inspection lot must permit the entry of the usage decision, the user must have the authorization to execute the Usage Decision function and any required certificate must have been received.

Q-112: C. Results have been recorded for required characteristics

A quality inspection is conducted to confirm the acceptability of a product for its intended purpose. During the inspection process, the results for inspection characteristics are recorded and compared with predefined quality requirements. On the basis of this comparison, individual characteristics are accepted or rejected. At the conclusion of the inspection, on the basis of inspection characteristic valuations, a usage decision is documented for the inspection lot. The entry of a usage decision for the inspection lot requires that inspection results have been documented for all required characteristics and for processed optional characteristics. In addition, the inspection lot must be released, the status of the inspection lot must permit the entry of the usage decision, the user must have the authorization to execute the Usage Decision function and any required certificate must have been received.

Q-113:   A. Confirmation of the receipt of a quality certificate, C. Release of inspection lot and D. User authorization for the transaction

A quality inspection is conducted to confirm the acceptability of a product for its intended purpose. During the inspection process, the results for inspection characteristics are recorded and compared with predefined quality requirements. On the basis of this comparison, individual characteristics are accepted or rejected. At the conclusion of the inspection, on the basis of inspection characteristic valuations, a usage decision is documented for the inspection lot. The entry of a usage decision for the inspection lot requires that inspection results have been documented for all required characteristics and for processed optional characteristics. In addition, the inspection lot must be released, the status of the inspection lot must permit the entry of the usage decision, the user must have the authorization to execute the Usage Decision function and any required certificate must have been received.

Q-114:   A. Status of the inspection lot is "Released" and C. Authorization to enter the usage decision

A quality inspection is conducted to confirm the acceptability of a product for its intended purpose. During the inspection process, the results for inspection characteristics are recorded and compared with predefined quality requirements. On the basis of this comparison, individual characteristics are accepted

or rejected. At the conclusion of the inspection, on the basis of inspection characteristic valuations, a usage decision is documented for the inspection lot. The entry of a usage decision for the inspection lot requires that inspection results have been documented for all required characteristics and for processed optional characteristics. In addition, the inspection lot must be released, the status of the inspection lot must permit the entry of the usage decision, the user must have the authorization to execute the Usage Decision function and any required certificate must have been received.

Q-115:   B. It is not necessary to record all inspection results for required inspection characteristics for the inspection lot prior to the entry of the usage decision

A quality inspection is conducted to determine the acceptability of a product for its intended purpose. A quality inspection is conducted to confirm the acceptability of a product for its intended purpose. During the inspection process, the results for inspection characteristics are recorded and compared with predefined quality requirements. On the basis of this comparison, individual characteristics are accepted or rejected. At the conclusion of the inspection, on the basis of inspection characteristic valuations, a usage decision is documented for the inspection lot. The entry of this usage decision typically requires the closure of all required characteristics and processed optional characteristics. However, it may be necessary to complete an inspection even if all inspection results have not been recorded for some required characteristics or some processed optional characteristics. In this case, the user has two options. The inspection can be completed with the Usage Decision - Complete Inspection function. In this instance, the status of the inspection lot is changed to "close completed." As an alternative, the short-term

185

characteristics can be closed by changing the status of the inspection lot to "short-term inspection completed" with the Usage Decision – Short-term Inspection function. In both cases, inspection results may not be revised unless the inspection lot status is reset.

Q-116:   A. Usage Decision - Overview of Defects

A quality inspection is conducted to confirm the acceptability of a product for its intended purpose. During the inspection process, the results for inspection characteristics are recorded and compared with predefined quality requirements. On the basis of this comparison, individual characteristics are accepted or rejected. At the conclusion of the inspection, on the basis of inspection characteristic valuations, a usage decision is documented for the inspection lot. As the usage decision is documented, other functions are automatically performed by the system. For example, a quality score for the inspection lot is calculated and a quality level data record, which determines inspection stages for a subsequent inspection lot, is updated. Also, the Quality Management Information System is updated and follow-up actions are executed. In addition to the automatic functions, the user may elect to perform other functions, as well. For example, the user can confirm activities for quality orders, activate quality notifications, create stock postings and create and display defect records that were confirmed for the inspection lot with the Overview of Defects, which displays information regarding the individual defects that influence a usage decision for an inspection lot. This overview displays the types of defects that were confirmed for an inspection lot and the defect structure.

Q-117:   B. The defects recorded for an inspection lot

A quality inspection is conducted to confirm the acceptability of a product for its intended purpose. During the inspection process, the results for inspection characteristics are recorded and compared with predefined quality requirements. On the basis of this comparison, individual characteristics are accepted or rejected. At the conclusion of the inspection, on the basis of inspection characteristic valuations, a usage decision is documented for the inspection lot. As the usage decision is documented, other functions are automatically performed by the system. For example, a quality score for the inspection lot is calculated and a quality level data record, which determines inspection stages for a subsequent inspection lot, is updated. Also, the Quality Management Information System is updated and follow-up actions are executed. In addition to the automatic functions, the user may elect to perform other functions, as well. For example, the user can confirm activities for quality orders, activate quality notifications, create stock postings and create and display defect records that were confirmed for the inspection lot with the Overview of Defects, which displays information regarding the individual defects that influence a usage decision for an inspection lot. This overview displays the types of defects that were confirmed for an inspection lot and the defect structure.

Q-118:   A. Usage Decision – Overview of Defects

A quality inspection is conducted to confirm the acceptability of a product for its intended purpose. During the inspection process, the results for inspection characteristics are recorded and compared with predefined quality requirements. On the basis of this comparison, individual characteristics are accepted or rejected. At the conclusion of the inspection, on the basis of inspection characteristic valuations, a usage decision is documented for the inspection lot. As the usage decision is documented, other functions are automatically performed by the system. For example, a quality score for the inspection lot is calculated and a quality level data record, which determines inspection stages for a subsequent inspection lot, is updated. Also, the Quality Management Information System is updated and follow-up actions are executed. In addition to the automatic functions, the user may elect to perform other functions, as well. For example, the user can confirm activities for quality orders, activate quality notifications, create stock postings and create and display defect records that were confirmed for the inspection lot with the Overview of Defects, which displays information regarding the individual defects that influence a usage decision for an inspection lot. This overview displays the types of defects that were confirmed for an inspection lot and the defect structure.

Q-119:   C. Usage Decision

A quality inspection is conducted to confirm the acceptability of a product for its intended purpose. During the inspection process, the results for inspection characteristics are recorded and compared with predefined quality requirements. On the basis of this comparison, individual characteristics are accepted or rejected. At the conclusion of the inspection, on the basis of inspection characteristic valuations, a usage decision is documented for the inspection lot. As the usage decision is documented, other functions are automatically performed by the system. For example, a quality score for the inspection lot is calculated and a quality level data record, which determines inspection stages for a subsequent inspection lot, is updated. Also, the Quality Management Information System is updated and follow-up actions are executed. In addition

to the automatic functions, the user may elect to perform other functions, as well. For example, the user can confirm activities for quality orders, activate quality notifications, create stock postings and create and display defect records that were confirmed for the inspection lot.

Q-120:   C. Initiate corrective action

A quality inspection is conducted to confirm the acceptability of a product for its intended purpose. During the inspection process, the results for inspection characteristics are recorded and compared with predefined quality requirements. On the basis of this comparison, individual characteristics are accepted or rejected. At the conclusion of the inspection, on the basis of inspection characteristic valuations, a usage decision is documented for the inspection lot. As the usage decision is documented, other functions are automatically performed by the system. For example, a quality score for the inspection lot is calculated and a quality level data record, which determines inspection stages for a subsequent inspection lot, is updated. Also, the Quality Management Information System is updated and follow-up actions are executed. In addition to the automatic functions, the user may elect to perform other functions, as well. For example, the user can create defect records, confirm activities for quality orders, create stock postings, record the number of defective units in the inspection lot or activate quality notifications, which will trigger corrective actions.

Q-121:   B. Entry of usage decision code

A quality inspection is conducted to confirm the acceptability of a product for its intended purpose. During the inspection process, the results for inspection characteristics are recorded and compared with predefined quality requirements. On the basis of

this comparison, individual characteristics are accepted or rejected. At the conclusion of the inspection, on the basis of inspection characteristic valuations, a usage decision is documented for the inspection lot. As the usage decision is documented, other functions are automatically performed by the system. For example, a quality score for the inspection lot is calculated and a quality level data record, which determines inspection stages for a subsequent inspection lot, is updated. Also, the Quality Management Information System is updated and follow-up actions are executed. In addition to the automatic functions, the user may elect to perform other functions, as well. For example, the user can create defect records, confirm activities for quality orders, create stock postings, record the number of defective units in the inspection lot or activate quality notifications, which will trigger corrective actions.

Q-122:   A. Quality score is calculated, C. Inspection lot status is updated and D. Subsequent entries to record inspection results can be made

A quality inspection is conducted to confirm the acceptability of a product for its intended purpose. During the inspection process, the results for inspection characteristics are recorded and compared with predefined quality requirements. On the basis of this comparison, individual characteristics are accepted or rejected. At the conclusion of the inspection, on the basis of inspection characteristic valuations, a usage decision is documented for the inspection lot. As the usage decision is documented, other functions are automatically performed by the system. For example, a quality score for the inspection lot is calculated and a quality level data record, which determines inspection stages for a subsequent inspection lot, is updated. Also, the Quality Management Information System is updated and follow-up actions are executed. In addition

to the automatic functions, the user may elect to perform other functions, as well. For example, the user can create defect records, confirm activities for quality orders, create stock postings, record the number of defective units in the inspection lot or activate quality notifications, which will trigger corrective actions.

Q-123: B. Background processing control indicator for the usage decision code and C. Stock proposal control indicator for the usage decision code

A quality inspection is conducted to confirm the acceptability of a product for its intended purpose. During the inspection process, the results for inspection characteristics are recorded and compared with predefined quality requirements. On the basis of this comparison, individual characteristics are accepted or rejected. At the conclusion of the inspection, on the basis of inspection characteristic valuations, a usage decision is documented for the inspection lot. In addition to the functionality required to record a usage decision, the Inspection Lot Completion component also includes the functionality necessary to enter stock postings for materials in a stock-relevant inspection lot. The user can post stock-relevant material before, after or simultaneous to the entry of the usage decision for the inspection lot. The account to which the stock is posted can be proposed by the system, on the basis of the Catalog type 3 usage decision code documented for the inspection lot. In addition, if the background processing control indicator is set in the usage decision set code, the stock is posted automatically to the appropriate account as the usage decision is recorded. In turn, the batch status control indicator in the usage decision code determines if the batch status is updated on the basis of the usage decision code and if so, if the status should be "restricted" or "unrestricted."

Q-124:   B. Overview of Characteristics

A quality inspection is conducted to confirm the acceptability of a product for its intended purpose. During the inspection process, the results for inspection characteristics are recorded and compared with predefined quality requirements. On the basis of this comparison, individual characteristics are accepted or rejected. At the conclusion of the inspection, on the basis of inspection characteristic valuations, a usage decision is documented for the inspection lot. To support inspection lot completion functions, the system provides four different overviews that are accessed by the Usage Decision function: the Overview of Characteristics, Overview of Defects, Overview of Inspection Points and Overview of Stocks. In particular, the Overview of Characteristics displays characteristic inspection results for an inspection lot and the status of the characteristics, which may indicate that results have yet to be recorded for some characteristics.

Q-125:   B. Activate quality notification

A quality inspection is conducted to confirm the acceptability of a product for its intended purpose. During the inspection process, the results for inspection characteristics are recorded and compared with predefined quality requirements. On the basis of this comparison, individual characteristics are accepted or rejected. At the conclusion of the inspection, on the basis of inspection characteristic valuations, a usage decision is documented for the inspection lot. As the usage decision is documented, other functions are automatically performed by the system. For example, a quality score for the inspection lot is calculated and a quality level data record, which determines inspection stages for a subsequent inspection lot, is updated. Also, the Quality Management Information System is updated and follow-up actions are executed. In addition to the automatic functions, the user may elect to perform other functions, as well. For example, the user can create defect records, confirm activities for quality orders, create stock postings, record the number of defective units in the inspection lot or activate quality notifications, which will trigger corrective actions.

Q-126:   B. Overview of Characteristics

A quality inspection is conducted to confirm the acceptability of a product for its intended purpose. During the inspection process, the results for inspection characteristics are recorded and compared with predefined quality requirements. On the basis of this comparison, individual characteristics are accepted or rejected. At the conclusion of the inspection, on the basis of inspection characteristic valuations, a usage decision is documented for the inspection lot. To support inspection lot completion functions, the system provides four different overviews that are accessed by the Usage Decision function: the Overview of Characteristics, Overview of Defects, Overview of Inspection Points and Overview of Stocks. In particular, the Overview of Characteristics displays characteristic inspection results for an inspection lot and the status of the characteristics, which may indicate that results have yet to be recorded for some characteristics.

Q-127:   B. Displays the inspection results for individual inspection characteristics in the inspection lot

A quality inspection is conducted to confirm the acceptability of a product for its intended purpose. During the inspection process, the results for inspection characteristics are recorded and compared

with predefined quality requirements. On the basis of this comparison, individual characteristics are accepted or rejected. At the conclusion of the inspection, on the basis of inspection characteristic valuations, a usage decision is documented for the inspection lot. To support inspection lot completion functions, the system provides four different overviews that are accessed by the Usage Decision function: the Overview of Characteristics, Overview of Defects, Overview of Inspection Points and Overview of Stocks. In particular, the Overview of Characteristics displays characteristic inspection results for an inspection lot and the status of the characteristics, which may indicate that results have yet to be recorded for some characteristics.

Q-128:   B. Display inspection results for a characteristic in chronological order

A quality inspection is conducted to confirm the acceptability of a product for its intended purpose. During the inspection process, the results for inspection characteristics are recorded and compared with predefined quality requirements. On the basis of this comparison, individual characteristics are accepted or rejected. At the conclusion of the inspection, on the basis of inspection characteristic valuations, a usage decision is documented for the inspection lot. As the usage decision is documented, other functions As a usage decision is documented, the system can display a summary of characteristic results that were documented for the particular inspection lot. In turn, characteristic results can be displayed in chronological order with the Results History function that is available by means of the Usage Decision or Results Recording functions.

Q-129:   D. All of the above

A stock posting documents the entry or removal of a manufactured or procured material to or from stock. The stock posting ensures that the material in a stock-relevant inspection lot is properly accounted for, which contributes to effective logistics management and financial propriety. The Inspection Lot Completion component includes the functionality necessary to make stock postings before, during or after a usage decision is recorded. For example, as a usage decision is recorded, the system can automatically propose a stock account to which the material in an inspection lot may be posted. For instance, material that is destroyed in an inspection can be posted to the sample usage stock account based on the control indicator that is set for usage decision code. As stock is posted, a material document is created with reference to the inspection lot. Data in the material document includes the quantity of material in an inspection lot, the quantity of material posted with a usage decision and the quantity of material transferred from storage location A to storage location B. Also included are the reason for the stock posting, the date the material document is created, the date of the stock posting, text and possibly a cost center.

Q-130:   B. Stock posting to scrap and C. Stock posting to blocked stock

A stock posting documents the entry or removal of a manufactured or procured material to or from stock. The stock posting ensures that the material in a stock-relevant inspection lot is properly accounted for, which contributes to effective logistics management and financial propriety. The Inspection Lot Completion component includes the functionality necessary to make stock postings before, during or after a usage decision is recorded. For example, as a usage decision is recorded, the system can automatically propose a stock account to which the material in an inspection lot may be posted. For instance, material that is destroyed in an inspection can be posted to the sample usage stock account based on the control indicator that is set for usage decision code. As stock is posted, a material document is created with reference to the inspection lot.

Q-131:   A. A manual or automatic process is used to make the stock posting and B. Postings in the Material Management component are made on the basis of stock postings entered in QM

A stock posting documents the entry or removal of a manufactured or procured material to or from stock. The stock posting ensures that the material in a stock-relevant inspection lot is properly accounted for, which contributes to effective logistics management and financial propriety. The Inspection Lot Completion component includes the functionality necessary to make stock postings before, during or after a usage decision is recorded.   For example, as a usage decision is recorded, the system can automatically propose a stock account to which the material in an inspection lot may be posted. For instance, material that is destroyed in an inspection can be posted to the sample usage stock account based on the control indicator that is set for usage decision code. As stock is posted using a manual or automatic process, a material document is created with reference to the inspection lot. The postings in the Material Management component are based on postings in the Quality Management component.

Q-132:   B. Inspection lot that is created with a manual process

A stock posting documents the entry or removal of a manufactured or procured material to or from stock.

196

The stock posting ensures that the material in a stock-relevant inspection lot is properly accounted for, which contributes to effective logistics management and financial propriety. The Inspection Lot Completion component includes the functionality necessary to make stock postings before, during or after a usage decision is recorded. For example, as a usage decision is recorded, the system can automatically propose a stock account to which the material in a stock-relevant inspection lot may be posted. As stock is posted, a material document is created with reference to the inspection lot. Inspection lots created using a manual process are not stock-relevant.

Q-133:   B. Usage Decision Results History

A quality inspection is conducted to confirm the acceptability of a product for its intended purpose. During the inspection process, the results for inspection characteristics are recorded and compared with predefined quality requirements. On the basis of this comparison, individual characteristics are accepted or rejected. At the conclusion of the inspection, on the basis of inspection characteristic valuations, a usage decision is documented for the inspection lot. As the usage decision is documented, other functions As a usage decision is documented, the system can display a summary of characteristic results that were documented for the particular inspection lot. In turn, characteristic results can be displayed in chronological order with the Results History function that is available by means of the Usage Decision or Results Recording functions.

Q-134:   A. Inspection lot quantity correction and B. Stock transfer

A stock posting documents the entry or removal of a manufactured or procured material to or from stock.

The stock posting ensures that the material in a stock-relevant inspection lot is properly accounted for, which contributes to effective logistics management and financial propriety. The Inspection Lot Completion component includes the functionality necessary to make stock postings before, during or after a usage decision is recorded. For example, as a usage decision is recorded, the system can automatically propose a stock account to which the material in an inspection lot may be posted. For instance, material that is destroyed in an inspection can be posted to the sample usage stock account based on the control indicator that is set for usage decision code. As stock is posted, a material document is created with reference to the inspection lot. A material document is also created in response to an inspection lot quantity correction or a stock transfer.

Q-135: A. Stock proposal control indicator for usage decision code and B. Background processing control indicator for usage decision code

A quality inspection is conducted to confirm the acceptability of a product for its intended purpose. During the inspection process, the results for inspection characteristics are recorded and compared with predefined quality requirements. On the basis of this comparison, individual characteristics are accepted or rejected. At the conclusion of the inspection, on the basis of inspection characteristic valuations, a usage decision is documented for the inspection lot. As the usage decision is documented, other functions are automatically performed by the system. For example, the system can enter stock postings for materials in a stock-relevant inspection lot. The user can post stock-relevant material before, after or simultaneous to the entry of the usage decision for the inspection lot. The account to which the stock is posted can be proposed by the system, on the basis of the Catalog type 3 usage decision code documented for the inspection lot. In addition, the stock is posted automatically to the appropriate account as the usage decision is recorded, if the background processing control indicator is set in the usage decision set code. In turn, the batch status control indicator in the usage decision code determines if the batch status is updated on the basis of the usage decision code and if so, if the status should be "restricted" or "unrestricted."

Q-136:   C. Usage decision set code

A quality inspection is conducted to confirm the acceptability of a product for its intended purpose. During the inspection process, the results for inspection characteristics are recorded and compared with predefined quality requirements. On the basis of this comparison, individual characteristics are accepted or rejected. At the conclusion of the inspection, on the basis of inspection characteristic valuations, a usage decision is documented for the inspection lot. The user can post stock-relevant material before, after or simultaneous to the entry of the usage decision for the inspection lot. If the background processing control indicator is set in the usage decision set code, the stock is posted automatically to the appropriate account as the usage decision is recorded.

Q-137:   A. Goods receipt document and B. Material document

A stock posting documents the entry or removal of a manufactured or procured material to or from stock. The stock posting ensures that the material in a stock-relevant inspection lot is properly accounted for, which contributes to effective logistics management and financial propriety. The Inspection Lot Completion component includes the functionality necessary to make stock postings before, during or after a usage decision is recorded. For example, as a usage decision is recorded, the system can automatically propose a stock account to which the material in an inspection lot may be posted. For instance, material that is destroyed in an inspection can be posted to the sample usage stock account based on the control indicator that is set for usage decision code. As stock is posted, a material document is created with reference to the inspection lot. In turn, a goods receipt document is created when an inspection lot is created.

Q-138:   A. Inspection lot number and C. Quantity of stock to be posted

A stock posting documents the entry or removal of a manufactured or procured material to or from stock. The stock posting ensures that the material in a stock-relevant inspection lot is properly accounted for, which contributes to effective logistics management and financial propriety. The Inspection Lot Completion component includes the functionality necessary to make stock postings before, during or after a usage decision is recorded. For example, as a usage decision is recorded, the system can automatically propose a stock account to which the material in an inspection lot may be posted. For instance, material that is destroyed in an inspection can be posted to the sample usage stock account based on the control indicator that is set for usage decision code. As stock is posted, a material document is created with reference to the inspection lot. The Inspection Lot Completion component Usage Decision function includes the functionality necessary to make stock postings after the usage decision for a lot has been posted. To do so, the user must specify an inspection lot number and the quantity of stock to be posted.

Q-139:   A. Ability to post stock for one inspection lot versus multiple inspection lots and B. Manual entry of stock posting versus use of worklist to post stocks.

A stock posting documents the entry or removal of a manufactured or procured material to or from stock. The stock posting ensures that the material in a stock-relevant inspection lot is properly accounted for, which contributes to effective logistics management and financial propriety. The Inspection Lot Completion component includes the functionality necessary to make stock postings before, during or after a usage decision is recorded. For example, as a usage decision is recorded, the system can automatically propose a stock account to which the material in an inspection lot may be posted. For instance, material that is destroyed in an inspection can be posted to the sample usage stock account based on the control indicator that is set for usage decision code. As stock is posted, a material document is created with reference to the inspection lot. The Inspection Lot Completion component Usage Decision function includes the functionality necessary to make stock postings after the usage decision for a lot has been posted. To do so, the user must specify an inspection lot number and the quantity of stock to be posted. When stock is posted after a usage decision is entered, a manual entry is used to post stock for one inspection lot whereas a worklist is used to post stock for several inspection lots.

Q-140:   A. Batch display, B. Batch where-used list and C. Post batch to new material

A quality inspection is conducted to confirm the acceptability of a product for its intended purpose. During the inspection process, the results for inspection characteristics are recorded and compared with predefined quality requirements. On the basis of

this comparison, individual characteristics are accepted or rejected. At the conclusion of the inspection, on the basis of inspection characteristic valuations, a usage decision is documented for the inspection lot. As the usage decision is documented, other functions are automatically performed by the system. For example, a quality score for the inspection lot is calculated and a quality level data record, which determines inspection stages for a subsequent inspection lot, is updated. Also, the Quality Management Information System is updated and follow-up actions are executed. In addition to the automatic functions, the user may elect to perform other functions, as well. For example, the user can create defect records, confirm activities for quality orders, activate quality notifications, create stock postings, and record the number of defective units in the inspection lot. The Inspection Lot Completion component also includes the functionality necessary to change the status of a batch, display batches for a particular material, create a batch where-used list, display batch characteristic values and post a batch to a material.

Q-141:   A. Creation of a serial number profile for movement type and B. Selection of single-unit inspection using serial numbers control indicator for material master inspection type

A stock posting documents the entry or removal of a manufactured or procured material to or from stock. The stock posting ensures that the material in a stock-relevant inspection lot is properly accounted for, which contributes to effective logistics management and financial propriety. The Inspection Lot Completion component includes the functionality necessary to make stock postings before, during or after a usage decision is recorded. For example, as a usage decision is recorded, the system can automatically propose a stock account , such as scrap or unrestricted use stock, to which the material in an inspection lot may be posted based on the control indicator that is set for usage decision code. As stock is posted, a material document is created with reference to the inspection lot. To post serialized material, a serial number profile for individual movement types is created and assigned to a material master record. Also required is the selection of the single-unit inspection with serial number inspection type in the material master record.

Q-142: D. All of the above

A stock posting documents the entry or removal of a manufactured or procured material to or from stock. The stock posting ensures that the material in a stock-relevant inspection lot is properly accounted for, which contributes to effective logistics management and financial propriety. The Inspection Lot Completion component includes the functionality necessary to make stock postings before, during or after a usage decision is recorded. For example, as a usage decision is recorded, the system can automatically propose a stock account , such as scrap or unrestricted use stock, to which the material in an inspection lot may be posted based on the control indicator that is set for usage decision code. As stock is posted, a material document is created with reference to the inspection lot. To post serialized material, a serial number profile for individual movement types is created and assigned to a material master record. Also required is the selection of the single-unit inspection with serial number inspection type in the material master record. In the process, you can post one or more units of serialized material to a number of different stock accounts, including return delivery, new material and scrap accounts. An object list that documents each posting of serialized materials to a stock account is then created and assigned to each individual material document.

Q-143:   C. Inspection lot record

A quality inspection is conducted to confirm the acceptability of a product for its intended purpose. During the inspection process, the results for inspection characteristics are recorded and compared with predefined quality requirements. On the basis of this comparison, individual characteristics are accepted or rejected. At the conclusion of the inspection, on the basis of inspection characteristic valuations, a usage decision is documented for the inspection lot. As the usage decision is documented, other functions are automatically performed by the system. For example, a quality score for the inspection lot is calculated and stored in the inspection lot record and a quality level data record, which determines inspection stages for a subsequent inspection lot, is updated. Also, the Quality Management Information System is updated and follow-up actions are executed.

Q-144:   A. Usage decision for inspection lot and C. Goods movement from inspection stock to unrestricted or blocked stock

A stock posting documents the entry or removal of a manufactured or procured material to or from stock. The stock posting ensures that the material in a stock-relevant inspection lot is properly accounted for, which contributes to effective logistics management and financial propriety. The Inspection Lot Completion component includes the functionality necessary to make stock postings before, during or after a usage decision is recorded. For example, as a usage decision is recorded, the system can automatically propose a stock account to which the material in an inspection lot may be posted. For instance, material that is destroyed in an inspection can be posted to the sample usage stock account based on the control indicator that is set for usage decision code. As stock is posted, a material document is created with reference to the inspection lot. In the event that a stock posting was made in error, it can be reversed. To do so requires the original entry of a usage decision for an inspection lot, a stock posting for the transfer of stock from inspection stock to unrestricted use stock, the creation of a return delivery with reference to the original purchase order and the cancellation of the inspection lot.

Q-145:   A. Menu option for Usage Decision function

A quality inspection is conducted to confirm the acceptability of a product for its intended purpose. During the inspection process, the results for inspection characteristics are recorded and compared with predefined quality requirements. On the basis of this comparison, individual characteristics are accepted or rejected. At the conclusion of the inspection, on the basis of inspection characteristic valuations, a usage decision is documented for the inspection lot. As the usage decision is documented, other functions are automatically performed by the system. For example, batch management functions can be performed such as revising a batch status and displaying a list of batches for a particular material. Also possible is the display of a batch where-used list, of batch characteristic values and posting a batch to a new material.

Q-146:   B. Create return delivery with reference to the original purchase order using the Inventory Management component

A stock posting documents the entry or removal of a manufactured or procured material to or from stock.

The stock posting ensures that the material in a stock-relevant inspection lot is properly accounted for, which contributes to effective logistics management and financial propriety. The Inspection Lot Completion component includes the functionality necessary to make stock postings before, during or after a usage decision is recorded. For example, as a usage decision is recorded, the system can automatically propose a stock account to which the material in an inspection lot may be posted. For instance, material that is destroyed in an inspection can be posted to the sample usage stock account based on the control indicator that is set for usage decision code. As stock is posted, a material document is created with reference to the inspection lot. In the event that a stock posting was made in error, it can be reversed. To do so requires the original entry of a usage decision for an inspection lot, a stock posting for the transfer of stock from inspection stock to unrestricted use stock, the creation of a return delivery with reference to the original purchase order and the cancellation of the inspection lot.

Q-147:   A. Serial number profile is not assigned to the material

A stock posting documents the entry of serialized parts or materials to or from stock. The stock posting ensures that the material in a stock-relevant inspection lot is properly accounted for, which contributes to effective logistics management and financial propriety. The Inspection Lot Completion component includes the functionality necessary to make stock postings before, during or after a usage decision is recorded. For example, as a usage decision is recorded, the system can automatically propose a stock account to which the material in an inspection lot may be posted. For instance, material that is destroyed in an inspection can be posted to the sample usage stock account based on the control indicator that is set for usage decision code. As stock is posted, a material document is created with reference to the inspection lot. This functionality requires the creation of a serial number profile for individual movement types and the assignment of the profile to a material master record. Also required is the selection of the single-unit inspection with serial number inspection type in the material master record.

Q-148:   B. Catalog for Usage Decisions #3

A quality inspection is conducted to confirm the acceptability of a product for its intended purpose. During the inspection process, the results for inspection characteristics are recorded and compared with predefined quality requirements. On the basis of this comparison, individual characteristics are accepted or rejected. At the conclusion of the inspection, on the basis of inspection characteristic valuations, a usage decision is documented for the inspection lot. Usage decision codes are maintained in the Usage Decision code catalog type 3.

Q-149:   C. Change batch status per the usage decision

A quality inspection is conducted to confirm the acceptability of a product for its intended purpose. During the inspection process, the results for inspection characteristics are recorded and compared with predefined quality requirements. On the basis of this comparison, individual characteristics are accepted or rejected. At the conclusion of the inspection, on the basis of inspection characteristic valuations, a usage decision is documented for the inspection lot. As the usage decision is documented, other functions are automatically performed by the system. For example, stock postings for materials in a stock-relevant inspection lot can be made. The user can post stock-relevant material before, after or simultaneous to the entry of the usage decision for the inspection lot. The system can propose the account to which the stock is posted on the basis of the Catalog type 3 usage decision code that's documented for the inspection lot. In addition, if the background processing control indicator is set in the usage decision set code, the stock is posted automatically to the appropriate account as the usage decision is recorded. In turn, the batch status control indicator in the usage decision code determines if the batch status is updated on the basis of the usage decision code and if so, if the status should be "restricted" or "unrestricted."

Q-150: A. Attach the results of a quality inspection to the batch determination procedure and B. Automatically valuate the general characteristics of the class using the measurement results of the closed characteristics

A quality inspection is conducted to confirm the acceptability of a product for its intended purpose. During the inspection process, the results for inspection characteristics are recorded and compared with predefined quality requirements. On the basis of this comparison, individual characteristics are accepted or rejected. At the conclusion of the inspection, on the basis of inspection characteristic valuations, a usage decision is documented for the inspection lot. As the usage decision is documented, other functions are automatically performed by the system. For example, batch management functions can be performed, such as revising a batch status, displaying a list of batches for a particular material, displaying a batch where-used list, displaying batch characteristic values and posting a batch to a new material. In addition, inspection results can be transferred to the batch class if the characteristics in the batch classification for a material are linked to characteristics. As a result, the characteristic results can be referenced by the batch determination procedure and class characteristics can be automatically valuated using inspection characteristic valuations.

Q-151:   A. Material is identified as a batch material in the material master, B. The master inspection characteristics are linked to the general characteristics in the classification system and C. The batch class was assigned to the material in the classification view of the material master

A quality inspection is conducted to confirm the acceptability of a product for its intended purpose. During the inspection process, the results for inspection characteristics are recorded and compared with predefined quality requirements. On the basis of this comparison, individual characteristics are accepted or rejected. At the conclusion of the inspection, on the basis of inspection characteristic valuations, a usage decision is documented for the inspection lot. As the usage decision is documented, other functions are automatically performed by the system. For example, batch management functions can be performed such as revising a batch status, displaying a list of batches for a particular material, displaying a batch where-used list, displaying batch characteristic values and posting a batch to a new material. In addition, inspection results can be transferred to the batch class if the characteristics in the batch classification for a material are linked to characteristics. As a result, the characteristic results can be referenced by the batch determination procedure and class characteristics can be automatically valuated using inspection characteristic valuations.

Q-152:   A. Recorded results can be changed before the usage decision is entered for an inspection lot

A quality inspection is conducted to confirm the acceptability of a product for its intended purpose. During the inspection process, the results for inspection characteristics are recorded and compared with predefined quality requirements. On the basis of this comparison, individual characteristics are accepted or rejected. At the conclusion of the inspection, on the basis of inspection characteristic valuations, a usage decision is documented for the inspection lot. Following the entry of inspection results, the recorded results can be changed before a usage decision is entered for an inspection lot or after the usage decision is entered if you change the usage decision with or without history.

Q-153:   A. Manual entry and C. Automatic entry based on material master record inspection type and algorithm

A quality inspection is conducted to confirm the acceptability of a product for its intended purpose. During the inspection process, the results for inspection characteristics are recorded and compared with predefined quality requirements. On the basis of this comparison, individual characteristics are accepted or rejected. At the conclusion of the inspection, on the basis of inspection characteristic valuations, a usage decision is documented for the inspection lot. As the usage decision is documented, other functions are automatically performed by the system. For example, a quality score for the inspection lot is calculated and a quality level data record, which determines inspection stages for a subsequent inspection lot, is updated. The procedure to calculate an inspection lot's quality score is defined for each inspection type and stored in the material master record. The quality score is calculated using certain criteria, such as the lot's usage decision code. Alternatively, a user can determine the lot's quality score using a manual process.

Q-154:   A. Inspection type

A quality inspection is conducted to confirm the acceptability of a product for its intended purpose. During the inspection process, the results for inspection characteristics are recorded and compared with predefined quality requirements. On the basis of this comparison, individual characteristics are accepted or rejected. At the conclusion of the inspection, on the basis of inspection characteristic valuations, a usage decision is documented for the inspection lot. As the usage decision is documented, other functions are automatically performed by the system. For example, a quality score for the inspection lot is calculated and a quality level data record, which determines inspection stages for a subsequent inspection lot, is updated. The process that calculates a quality score is defined for each inspection type and stored in the material master record. The score can be automatically calculated using certain criteria, such as the lot's usage decision code. Alternatively, a user can determine the lot's quality score using a manual process.

Q-155:   C. Algorithm assigned to material master inspection type and D. Share of defects for characteristics

A quality inspection is conducted to confirm the acceptability of a product for its intended purpose. During the inspection process, the results for inspection characteristics are recorded and compared with predefined quality requirements. On the basis of this comparison, individual characteristics are accepted or rejected. At the conclusion of the inspection, on the basis of inspection characteristic valuations, a usage decision is documented for the inspection lot. As the

usage decision is documented, other functions are automatically performed by the system. For example, a quality score for the inspection lot is calculated and a quality level data record, which determines inspection stages for a subsequent inspection lot, is updated. The process that calculates a quality score is defined for each inspection type and stored in the material master record. The score can be automatically calculated using certain criteria, such as the lot's usage decision code. Alternatively, a user can determine the lot's quality score using a manual process.

Q-156:   B. Quality score is derived using algorithm defined in material master record inspection type

A quality inspection is conducted to confirm the acceptability of a product for its intended purpose. During the inspection process, the results for inspection characteristics are recorded and compared with predefined quality requirements. On the basis of this comparison, individual characteristics are accepted or rejected. At the conclusion of the inspection, on the basis of inspection characteristic valuations, a usage decision is documented for the inspection lot. As the usage decision is documented, other functions are automatically performed by the system. For example, a quality score for the inspection lot is calculated and a quality level data record, which determines inspection stages for a subsequent inspection lot, is updated. A user can enter a quality score using a manual process or the system can automatically calculate the score using a predefined process defined for the inspection type defined in the material master record. The quality score for a material can be based on a number of criteria, including the usage decision code that is documented for an inspection lot.

Q-157:   A. Inspection plan is used to inspect the materials and B. Defect classes are assigned to defect codes

A quality inspection is conducted to confirm the acceptability of a product for its intended purpose. During the inspection process, the results for inspection characteristics are recorded and compared with predefined quality requirements. On the basis of this comparison, individual characteristics are accepted or rejected. At the conclusion of the inspection, on the basis of inspection characteristic valuations, a usage decision is documented for the inspection lot. As the usage decision is documented, other functions are automatically performed by the system. For example, a quality score for the inspection lot is calculated and a quality level data record, which determines inspection stages for a subsequent inspection lot, is updated. A user can enter a quality score using a manual process or the system can automatically calculate the score using a predefined process defined for the inspection type defined in the material master record. The quality score for a material can be based on a number of criteria, including the usage decision code that is documented for an inspection lot. To calculate the quality score automatically requires that the inspection be conducted with an inspection plan and that defect classes are assigned to defect codes.

Q-158:   C. Quality score can be calculated per algorithm defined in material master record inspection type

A quality inspection is conducted to confirm the acceptability of a product for its intended purpose. During the inspection process, the results for inspection characteristics are recorded and compared with predefined quality requirements. On the basis of this comparison, individual characteristics are accepted

or rejected. At the conclusion of the inspection, on the basis of inspection characteristic valuations, a usage decision is documented for the inspection lot. As the usage decision is documented, other functions are automatically performed by the system. For example, a quality score for the inspection lot is calculated and a quality level data record, which determines inspection stages for a subsequent inspection lot, is updated.

Q-159:   A. Manual procedure to enter quality score and C. Automatic procedure to enter a quality score on the basis of the inspection type and the usage decision code

A quality inspection is conducted to confirm the acceptability of a product for its intended purpose. During the inspection process, the results for inspection characteristics are recorded and compared with predefined quality requirements. On the basis of this comparison, individual characteristics are accepted or rejected. At the conclusion of the inspection, on the basis of inspection characteristic valuations, a usage decision is documented for the inspection lot. As the usage decision is documented, other functions are automatically performed by the system. For example, a quality score for the inspection lot is calculated and a quality level data record, which determines inspection stages for a subsequent inspection lot, is updated. The procedure used to automatically calculate the inspection lot's quality score is defined for each inspection type and stored in the material master record. The score is automatically calculated using certain criteria, such as the lot's usage decision code. Alternatively, a user can determine the lot's quality score using a manual process.

Q-160:   B. Quality score can be calculated with procedure or defined for usage decision code

A quality inspection is conducted to confirm the acceptability of a product for its intended purpose. During the inspection process, the results for inspection characteristics are recorded and compared with predefined quality requirements. On the basis of this comparison, individual characteristics are accepted or rejected. At the conclusion of the inspection, on the basis of inspection characteristic valuations, a usage decision is documented for the inspection lot. As the usage decision is documented, other functions are automatically performed by the system. For example, a quality score for the inspection lot is calculated and a quality level data record, which determines inspection stages for a subsequent inspection lot, is updated. The procedure used to automatically calculate the inspection lot's quality score is defined for each inspection type and stored in the material master record. The score is automatically calculated using certain criteria, such as the lot's usage decision code. Alternatively, a user can determine the lot's quality score using a manual process. The upper and lower limits for the score are defined using the Customizing application.

Q-161:   C. Customizing application

A quality inspection is conducted to confirm the acceptability of a product for its intended purpose. During the inspection process, the results for inspection characteristics are recorded and compared with predefined quality requirements. On the basis of this comparison, individual characteristics are accepted or rejected. At the conclusion of the inspection, on the basis of inspection characteristic valuations, a usage decision is documented for the inspection lot. As the usage decision is documented, other functions are automatically performed by the system. For example, a quality score for the inspection lot is calculated and a quality level data record, which determines inspection stages for a subsequent inspection lot, is updated. The procedure used to automatically calculate the inspection lot's quality score is defined for each inspection type and stored in the material master record. The score is automatically calculated using certain criteria, such as the lot's usage decision code. Alternatively, a user can determine the lot's quality score using a manual process. The upper and lower limits for the score are defined using the Customizing application.

Q-162:   B. Data used in calculation of a quality score for an inspection lot

A quality inspection is conducted to confirm the acceptability of a product for its intended purpose. During the inspection process, the results for inspection characteristics are recorded and compared with predefined quality requirements. On the basis of this comparison, individual characteristics are accepted or rejected. At the conclusion of the inspection, on the basis of inspection characteristic valuations, a usage decision is documented for the inspection lot. As the usage decision is documented, other functions are automatically performed by the system. For example, a quality score for the inspection lot is calculated using criteria such as share of defects for characteristics or a usage decision code and a quality level data record, which determines inspection stages for a subsequent inspection lot, is updated. Also, the Quality Management Information System is updated and follow-up actions are executed.

Q-163:   B. Algorithm to calculate quality score for material master record inspection type and C. Quality score assigned to group code in Usage Decision catalog

A quality inspection is conducted to confirm the acceptability of a product for its intended purpose.

During the inspection process, the results for inspection characteristics are recorded and compared with predefined quality requirements. On the basis of this comparison, individual characteristics are accepted or rejected. At the conclusion of the inspection, on the basis of inspection characteristic valuations, a usage decision is documented for the inspection lot. As the usage decision is documented, other functions are automatically performed by the system. For example, a quality score for the inspection lot is calculated and a quality level data record, which determines inspection stages for a subsequent inspection lot, is updated. The quality score for a material is calculated on the basis of a number of criteria including the usage decision code that is documented for an inspection lot. A user can enter a quality score using a manual process or the system can automatically calculate the score using a predefined process defined for the inspection type defined in the material master record. Share of defects for characteristics and usage decision code are examples of data used in calculation of a quality score for an inspection lot.

Q-164:   B. Record usage decision

A quality inspection is conducted to confirm the acceptability of a product for its intended purpose. During the inspection process, the results for inspection characteristics are recorded and compared with predefined quality requirements. On the basis of this comparison, individual characteristics are accepted or rejected. At the conclusion of the inspection, on the basis of inspection characteristic valuations, a usage decision is documented for the inspection lot. As the usage decision is documented, other functions are automatically performed by the system. For example, a quality score for the inspection lot is calculated and a quality level data record, which determines inspection stages for a subsequent inspection lot, is updated. Also, the Quality Management Information System is updated and follow-up actions are executed. In addition to the automatic functions, the user may elect to perform other functions, as well. For example, the user can create defect records, confirm activities for quality orders, activate quality notifications, create stock postings, and record the number of defective units in the inspection lot.

Q-165:   B. Vendor evaluation and C. Vendor letter of complaint

A quality inspection is conducted to confirm the acceptability of a product for its intended purpose. During the inspection process, the results for inspection characteristics are recorded and compared with predefined quality requirements. On the basis of this comparison, individual characteristics are accepted or rejected. At the conclusion of the inspection, on the basis of inspection characteristic valuations, a usage decision is documented for the inspection lot. As the usage decision is documented, other functions are automatically performed by the system. For example, a quality score for the inspection lot is calculated and a quality level data record, which determines inspection stages for a subsequent inspection lot, is updated. Also, the Quality Management Information System is updated and follow-up actions are executed. In addition to the automatic functions, the user may elect to perform other functions, as well. For example, the user can confirm activities for quality orders, activate quality notifications, create and reverse stock postings and create and display defect records that were confirmed for the inspection lot. The confirmed defective quantity for an inspection lot is used for vendor evaluations and vendor letters of complaint.

Q-166:   B. The procedure used to automatically calculate a quality score can be defined and activated when inspection type is activated and C. A quality score can be based on the share of defects for each characteristic or for the inspection lot

A quality inspection is conducted to confirm the acceptability of a product for its intended purpose. During the inspection process, the results for inspection characteristics are recorded and compared with predefined quality requirements. On the basis of this comparison, individual characteristics are accepted or rejected. At the conclusion of the inspection, on the basis of inspection characteristic valuations, a usage decision is documented for the inspection lot. As the usage decision is documented, other functions are automatically performed by the system. For example, a quality score for the inspection lot is calculated and a quality level data record, which determines inspection stages for a subsequent inspection lot, is updated.
The quality score is a statistical value that represents the quality of a material in an inspection lot. The score might be gauged by the adherence of the characteristics of a material to predefined specifications and represented by a usage decision code. Alternatively, the score might be based on the share of defects recorded for an inspection lot or inspection characteristics, or the quality score for inspection characteristics. Consequently, a quality score can be predefined for each usage decision code or calculated by the system. If the system determines the quality score, it is calculated according to a procedure defined for an inspection type and documented in the material master.

Q-167:   A. All inspected characteristics of the inspection lot are accepted, B. All required inspection characteristics are confirmed and closed and C. No defect records were created for the inspection lot

A quality inspection is conducted to confirm the acceptability of a product for its intended purpose. During the inspection process, the results for inspection characteristics are recorded and compared with predefined quality requirements. On the basis of this comparison, individual characteristics are accepted or rejected. At the conclusion of the inspection, on the basis of inspection characteristic valuations, a usage decision is documented for the inspection lot. The entry of a usage decision requires that inspection results have been documented for all required characteristics and for processed optional characteristics. In addition, the inspection lot must be released, the status of the inspection lot must permit the entry of the usage decision, the user must have the authorization to execute the Usage Decision function and any required certificate must have been received. In turn, the usage decision for the inspection lot can be recorded irrespective of unevaluated inspection points.

Q-168:   D. All inspection characteristics in inspection lot are accepted

A quality inspection is conducted to confirm the acceptability of a product for its intended purpose. During the inspection process, the results for inspection characteristics are recorded and compared with predefined quality requirements. On the basis of this comparison, individual characteristics are accepted or rejected. At the conclusion of the inspection, on the basis of inspection characteristic valuations, a usage decision is documented for the inspection lot. The entry of a usage decision requires that inspection results have been documented for all required characteristics and for processed optional characteristics. In addition, the inspection lot must be released, the status of the inspection lot must permit the entry of the usage decision, the user must have the authorization to execute the Usage Decision function and any required certificate must have been received. In turn, the usage decision for the inspection lot can be recorded irrespective of unevaluated inspection points.

Q-169:   A. Share of defects in lot

A quality inspection is conducted to confirm the acceptability of a product for its intended purpose. During the inspection process, the results for inspection characteristics are recorded and compared with predefined quality requirements. On the basis of this comparison, individual characteristics are accepted or rejected. At the conclusion of the inspection, on the basis of inspection characteristic valuations, a usage decision is documented for the inspection lot. As the usage decision is documented, other functions are automatically performed by the system. For example, a quality score for the inspection lot is calculated and a quality level data record, which determines inspection stages for a subsequent inspection lot, is updated.
An inspection lot's quality score is a statistical value that represents the quality of a material in an inspection lot as gauged by the adherence of the characteristics of a material to predefined specifications. This method the system uses to automatically calculate the quality score is defined for each inspection type and stored in the material master record. A lot's quality score is calculated using certain criteria, such as the lot's usage decision code. The quality score also can be based on the share of defects recorded for an inspection lot or inspection characteristics. Alternatively, a user can determine the lot's quality score using a manual process.

Q-170:   B. Determine if a material in an inspection lot is accepted or rejected for its intended purpose

A quality inspection is conducted to confirm the acceptability of a product for its intended purpose. During the inspection process, the results for

inspection characteristics are recorded and compared with predefined quality requirements. On the basis of this comparison, individual characteristics are accepted or rejected. At the conclusion of the inspection, on the basis of inspection characteristic valuations, a usage decision is documented for the inspection lot. The usage decision determines if a material is accepted or rejected for its intended purpose.

Q-171:   A. Required characteristics are not valuated

A quality inspection is conducted to confirm the acceptability of a product for its intended purpose. During the inspection process, the results for inspection characteristics are recorded and compared with predefined quality requirements. On the basis of this comparison, individual characteristics are accepted or rejected. At the conclusion of the inspection, on the basis of inspection characteristic valuations, a usage decision is documented for the inspection lot.
The entry of this usage decision typically requires the closure of all required characteristics and processed optional characteristics. However, it may be necessary to complete an inspection even if all inspection results have not been recorded for some required characteristics or some processed optional characteristics. In this case, the user has two options. The inspection can be completed with the Usage Decision - Complete Inspection function. In this instance, the status of the inspection lot is changed to "close completed." As an alternative, the short-term characteristics can be closed by changing the status of the inspection lot to "short-term inspection completed" with the Usage Decision – Short-term Inspection function. In both cases, inspection results may not be revised unless the inspection lot status is reset.

Q-172:   A. Times for activity types can be confirmed to a QM order

A quality inspection is conducted to confirm the acceptability of a product for its intended purpose. During the inspection process, the results for inspection characteristics are recorded and compared with predefined quality requirements. On the basis of this comparison, individual characteristics are accepted or rejected. At the conclusion of the inspection, on the basis of inspection characteristic valuations, a usage decision is documented for the inspection lot. As the usage decision is documented, other functions are automatically performed by the system. For example, a quality score for the inspection lot is calculated and a quality level data record, which determines inspection stages for a subsequent inspection lot, is updated. Also, the Quality Management Information System is updated and follow-up actions are executed. In addition to the automatic functions, the user may elect to perform other functions, as well. For example, the user can create defect records, confirm activities for quality orders, activate quality notifications, create stock postings, and record the number of defective units in the inspection lot.

Q-173:   C. Material master record

A quality inspection is conducted to confirm the acceptability of a product for its intended purpose. During the inspection process, the results for inspection characteristics are recorded and compared with predefined quality requirements. On the basis of this comparison, individual characteristics are accepted or rejected. At the conclusion of the inspection, on the basis of inspection characteristic valuations, a usage decision is documented for the inspection lot. As the usage decision is documented, other functions are automatically performed by the system. For example, batch management functions can be performed such as

223

revising a batch status, displaying a list of batches for a particular material, displaying a batch where-used list, displaying batch characteristic values and posting a batch to a new material. In addition, inspection results can be transferred to the batch class if the characteristics in the batch classification for a material are linked to characteristics. As a result, the characteristic results can be referenced by the batch determination procedure and class characteristics can be automatically valuated using inspection characteristic valuations. A material is identified as a batch material in the material master record.

Q-174:   A. Quality level for current inspection lot is updated and C. The recorded results for a characteristic cannot be changed

A quality inspection is conducted to confirm the acceptability of a product for its intended purpose. During the inspection process, the results for inspection characteristics are recorded and compared with predefined quality requirements. On the basis of this comparison, individual characteristics are accepted or rejected. At the conclusion of the inspection, on the basis of inspection characteristic valuations, a usage decision is documented for the inspection lot. As the usage decision is documented, other functions are automatically performed by the system. For example, a quality score for the inspection lot is calculated and a quality level data record, which determines inspection stages for a subsequent inspection lot, is updated. In addition, the Quality Management Information System is updated and follow-up actions are executed. After the inspection lot is completed, characteristic results can't be changed.

Q-175:   A. Complete inspection with open characteristics and B. Complete inspection on short-term basis

A quality inspection is conducted to confirm the acceptability of a product for its intended purpose. During the inspection process, the results for inspection characteristics are recorded and compared with predefined quality requirements. On the basis of this comparison, individual characteristics are accepted or rejected. At the conclusion of the inspection, on the basis of inspection characteristic valuations, a usage decision is documented for the inspection lot. As the usage decision is documented, other functions are automatically performed by the system. If it's necessary to complete an inspection if inspection results have not been recorded for all required characteristics or processed optional characteristics, the user has two options. The inspection can be completed with the Usage Decision - Complete Inspection function. In this instance, the status of the inspection lot is changed to "close completed." As an alternative, the short-term characteristics can be closed by changing the status of the inspection lot to "short-term inspection completed" with the Usage Decision – Short-term Inspection function. In both cases, inspection results may not be revised unless the inspection lot status is reset.

Q-176:   B. Discontinue inspection and C. Valuate inspection points and enter usage decision

A quality inspection is conducted to confirm the acceptability of a product for its intended purpose. During the inspection process, the results for inspection characteristics are recorded and compared with predefined quality requirements. On the basis of this comparison, individual characteristics are accepted or rejected. At the conclusion of the inspection, on the basis of inspection characteristic valuations, a usage decision is documented for the inspection lot. As the

usage decision is documented, other functions are automatically performed by the system. For example, If it's necessary to complete an inspection if inspection results have not been recorded for all inspection points, the user has two options. The user can discontinue the inspection or valuate inspection points and enter usage decision.

Q-177:   A. Create Usage Decision function and B. Change Usage Decision function

A quality inspection is conducted to confirm the acceptability of a product for its intended purpose. During the inspection process, the results for inspection characteristics are recorded and compared with predefined quality requirements. On the basis of this comparison, individual characteristics are accepted or rejected. At the conclusion of the inspection, on the basis of inspection characteristic valuations, a usage decision is documented for the inspection lot. As the usage decision is documented, other functions are automatically performed by the system. For example, a quality score for the inspection lot is calculated and a quality level data record, which determines inspection stages for a subsequent inspection lot, is updated. Also, the Quality Management Information System is updated and follow-up actions are executed. In addition to the automatic functions, the user may elect to perform other functions, as well. For example, the user can create defect records, confirm activities for quality orders, activate quality notifications, create stock postings, and record the number of defective units in the inspection lot. A user can also access a display of the inspection points that exist for an inspection lot with the Record, Change or Display Usage Decision functions.

Q-178:   A. Production quantities, B. Physical samples and C. Equipment

226

A quality inspection is conducted to confirm the acceptability of a product for its intended purpose. During the inspection process, the results for inspection characteristics are recorded and compared with predefined quality requirements. On the basis of this comparison, individual characteristics are accepted or rejected. At the conclusion of the inspection, on the basis of inspection characteristic valuations, a usage decision is documented for the inspection lot. As the usage decision is documented, other functions are automatically performed by the system. For example, a quality score for the inspection lot is calculated and a quality level data record, which determines inspection stages for a subsequent inspection lot, is updated. Also, the Quality Management Information System is updated and follow-up actions are executed. In addition to the automatic functions, the user may elect to perform other functions, as well. For example, the user can create defect records, confirm activities for quality orders, activate quality notifications, create stock postings, and record the number of defective units in the inspection lot. A user can also access a display of the inspection points that exist for production quantities, physical samples and equipment with the Record, Change or Display Usage Decision functions.

Q-179:   A. Results recorded for all required inspection characteristics and B. Receipt of required quality certificate

A quality inspection is conducted to confirm the acceptability of a product for its intended purpose. During the inspection process, the results for inspection characteristics are recorded and compared with predefined quality requirements. On the basis of this comparison, individual characteristics are accepted or rejected. At the conclusion of the inspection, on the

basis of inspection characteristic valuations, a usage decision is documented for the inspection lot. The entry of a usage decision for the inspection lot requires that inspection results have been documented for all required characteristics and for processed optional characteristics. In addition, the inspection lot must be released, the status of the inspection lot must permit the entry of the usage decision, the user must have the authorization to execute the Usage Decision function and any required certificate must have been received.

Q-180:   C. Usage Decision function authorization and D. Release of inspection lot

A quality inspection is conducted to confirm the acceptability of a product for its intended purpose. During the inspection process, the results for inspection characteristics are recorded and compared with predefined quality requirements. On the basis of this comparison, individual characteristics are accepted or rejected. At the conclusion of the inspection, on the basis of inspection characteristic valuations, a usage decision is documented for the inspection lot. The entry of a usage decision for the inspection lot requires that inspection results have been documented for all required characteristics and for processed optional characteristics. In addition, the inspection lot must be released, the status of the inspection lot must permit the entry of the usage decision, the user must have the authorization to execute the Usage Decision function and any required certificate must have been received.

Q-181:   C. Receipt of quality certificate must be confirmed prior to entry of usage decision

A quality inspection is conducted to confirm the acceptability of a product for its intended purpose.

228

During the inspection process, the results for inspection characteristics are recorded and compared with predefined quality requirements. On the basis of this comparison, individual characteristics are accepted or rejected. At the conclusion of the inspection, on the basis of inspection characteristic valuations, a usage decision is documented for the inspection lot. The entry of a usage decision for the inspection lot requires that inspection results have been documented for all required characteristics and for processed optional characteristics. In addition, the inspection lot must be released, the status of the inspection lot must permit the entry of the usage decision, the user must have the authorization to execute the Usage Decision function and any required certificate must have been received.

Q-182:   A. Usage Decision - Display Defect Structure

A quality inspection is conducted to confirm the acceptability of a product for its intended purpose. During the inspection process, the results for inspection characteristics are recorded and compared with predefined quality requirements. On the basis of this comparison, individual characteristics are accepted or rejected. At the conclusion of the inspection, on the basis of inspection characteristic valuations, a usage decision is documented for the inspection lot. The system also provides four different overviews that are accessed by the Usage Decision function that support the Inspection Lot Completion transactions: Overview of Characteristics, Overview of Defects, Overview of Inspection Points and Overview of Stocks. In particular, the Overview of Defects displays information regarding the individual defects that impact a usage decision for an inspection lot. This overview displays the types of defects that were confirmed for an inspection lot and the defect structure, as well as provides a means to activate a quality notification.

Q-183:   A. Usage Decision - Display Defect Structure

A quality inspection is conducted to confirm the acceptability of a product for its intended purpose. During the inspection process, the results for inspection characteristics are recorded and compared with predefined quality requirements. On the basis of this comparison, individual characteristics are accepted or rejected. At the conclusion of the inspection, on the basis of inspection characteristic valuations, a usage decision is documented for the inspection lot. The system also provides four different overviews that are accessed by the Usage Decision function that support the Inspection Lot Completion transactions: Overview of Characteristics, Overview of Defects, Overview of Inspection Points and Overview of Stocks. In particular, the Overview of Defects displays information regarding the individual defects that impact a usage decision for an inspection lot. This overview displays the types of defects that were confirmed for an inspection lot and the defect structure, as well as provides a means to activate a quality notification.

Q-184:   C. Stock proposal control indicator for usage decision code

A stock posting documents the entry or removal of a manufactured or procured material to or from stock. The stock posting ensures that the material in a stock-relevant inspection lot is properly accounted for, which contributes to effective logistics management and financial propriety. The Inspection Lot Completion component includes the functionality necessary to make stock postings before, during or after a usage decision is recorded.   For example, as a usage decision is recorded, the system can automatically propose a stock account to which the material in an inspection lot may be posted on the basis of control indicators in the usage decision codes. For instance, material that is destroyed in an inspection can be posted to the sample usage stock account based on the control indicator that is set for usage decision code. As stock is posted, a material document is created with reference to the inspection lot. The stock proposal requires the selection of the stock proposal control indicator in catalog type 3 set code and the background processing control indicator in catalog type 3 set code. The usage decision codes may be defined for a selected set that is defined for an inspection type or for the inspection catalog type 3.

Q-185: A. Usage Decision - Overview of Stocks

A stock posting documents the entry or removal of a manufactured or procured material to or from stock. The stock posting ensures that the material in a stock-relevant inspection lot is properly accounted for, which contributes to effective logistics management and financial propriety. The Inspection Lot Completion component includes the functionality necessary to view stock in the inspection lot and then post the inspected materials to the appropriate stock account. The Usage Decision – Overview of Stocks is used for this purpose.

Q-186: C. Assignment of QM order to a material

A quality inspection is conducted to confirm the acceptability of a product for its intended purpose. During the inspection process, the results for inspection characteristics are recorded and compared with predefined quality requirements. On the basis of this comparison, individual characteristics are accepted or rejected. At the conclusion of the inspection, on the basis of inspection characteristic valuations, a usage decision is documented for the inspection lot. As the usage decision is documented, other functions are automatically performed by the system. For example, a

quality score for the inspection lot is calculated and a quality level data record, which determines inspection stages for a subsequent inspection lot, is updated. Also, the Quality Management Information System is updated and follow-up actions are executed. In addition to the automatic functions, the user may elect to perform other functions, as well. For example, the user can create defect records, confirm activities for quality orders, activate quality notifications, create stock postings, and record the number of defective units in the inspection lot. The confirmation of values for activity types to a QM order requires the assignment of the QM order to a material.

Q-187:   A. Destructive inspection for characteristic control indicator

A stock posting documents the entry or removal of a manufactured or procured material to or from stock. The stock posting ensures that the material in a stock-relevant inspection lot is properly accounted for, which contributes to effective logistics management and financial propriety. The Inspection Lot Completion component includes the functionality necessary to make stock postings before, during or after a usage decision is recorded. For example, as a usage decision is recorded, the system can automatically propose a stock account to which the material in an inspection lot may be posted. As the stock postings are made, the quantity of material destroyed during the inspection can be calculated. The system can then create a stock posting proposal to post this quantity to the sample usage account. This function requires the activation of the destructive inspection control indicator for any inspection characteristic for which material is to be posted to the sample usage account. Stock postings for a destructive inspection can occur simultaneously with the automatic entry of the usage decision or the manual entry of the usage decision with automatic stock postings.

Q-188:   A. Results recording process and B. Usage decision process

A quality inspection is conducted to confirm the acceptability of a product for its intended purpose. During the inspection process, the results for inspection characteristics are recorded and compared with predefined quality requirements. On the basis of this comparison, individual characteristics are accepted or rejected. At the conclusion of the inspection, on the basis of inspection characteristic valuations, a usage decision is documented for the inspection lot. As the usage decision is documented, other functions are automatically performed by the system. For example, a quality score for the inspection lot is calculated and a quality level data record, which determines inspection stages for a subsequent inspection lot, is updated. Also, the Quality Management Information System is updated and follow-up actions are executed. In addition to the automatic functions, the user may elect to perform other functions, as well. For example, the user can create defect records, confirm activities for quality orders, activate quality notifications, create stock postings, and record the number of defective units in the inspection lot. Stock postings can be posted using the Results Recording or Usage Decision functions.

Q-189:   A. Batch classification data will be displayed in the usage decision log

A quality inspection is conducted to confirm the acceptability of a product for its intended purpose. During the inspection process, the results for inspection characteristics are recorded and compared with predefined quality requirements. On the basis of

this comparison, individual characteristics are accepted or rejected. At the conclusion of the inspection, on the basis of inspection characteristic valuations, a usage decision is documented for the inspection lot. In addition to the functionality required to record a usage decision, the Inspection Lot Completion component also includes the functionality necessary to change the status of a batch, display batches for a particular material, create a batch where-used list, display batch characteristic values and post a batch to a material. If a usage decision and quality score for an inspection lot is transferred to the batch classification, the batch classification data will be displayed in the usage decision log.

Q-190:   A. Usage Decision function

A quality inspection is conducted to confirm the acceptability of a product for its intended purpose. During the inspection process, the results for inspection characteristics are recorded and compared with predefined quality requirements. On the basis of this comparison, individual characteristics are accepted or rejected. At the conclusion of the inspection, on the basis of inspection characteristic valuations, a usage decision is documented for the inspection lot. As the usage decision is documented, other functions are automatically performed by the system. For example, the Inspection Lot Completion component also includes the functionality necessary to change the status of a batch, display batches for a particular material, create a batch where-used list, display batch characteristic values and post a batch to a material. If a usage decision and quality score for an inspection lot is transferred to the batch classification, the batch classification data will be displayed in the usage decision log.

Q-191: A. Display a cost report

A quality inspection is conducted to confirm the acceptability of a product for its intended purpose. During the inspection process, the results for inspection characteristics are recorded and compared with predefined quality requirements. On the basis of this comparison, individual characteristics are accepted or rejected. At the conclusion of the inspection, on the basis of inspection characteristic valuations, a usage decision is documented for the inspection lot. As the usage decision is documented, other functions are automatically performed by the system. For example, a quality score for the inspection lot is calculated and a quality level data record, which determines inspection stages for a subsequent inspection lot, is updated. Also, the Quality Management Information System is updated and follow-up actions are executed. In addition to the automatic functions, the user may elect to perform other functions, as well. For example, the user can create defect records, activate quality notifications, create stock postings, record the number of defective units in the inspection lot or confirm activities for quality orders. In addition, with the Change Usage Decision function, the user can display a cost report to review confirmation values debited to the QM order.

Q-192: A. Client

A quality inspection is conducted to confirm the acceptability of a produc33t for its intended purpose. During the inspection process, the results for inspection characteristics are recorded and compared with predefined quality requirements. On the basis of this comparison, individual characteristics are accepted or rejected. At the conclusion of the inspection, on the basis of inspection characteristic valuations, a usage decision is documented for the inspection lot. As the usage decision is documented, other functions are automatically performed by the system. For example, a quality score for the inspection lot is calculated and a quality level data record, which determines inspection stages for a subsequent inspection lot, is updated. The method used to calculate a quality score is defined for each inspection type and stored in the material master record. This calculation uses certain criteria, such as the lot's usage decision code. Alternatively, a user can determine the lot's quality score using a manual process. In either case, the upper and lower limits of a quality score are defined at the client level.

Q-193:   B. Usage decision code

A stock posting documents the entry or removal of a manufactured or procured material to or from stock. The stock posting ensures that the material in a stock-relevant inspection lot is properly accounted for, which contributes to effective logistics management and financial propriety. The Inspection Lot Completion component includes the functionality necessary to make stock postings before, during or after a usage decision is recorded. For example, as a usage decision is recorded, the system can automatically propose a stock account to which the material in an inspection lot may be posted. For instance, material that is destroyed in an inspection can be posted to the sample usage stock account based on the control indicator that is set for usage decision code. As stock is posted, a material document is created with reference to the inspection lot.

Q-194:   Usage Decision - Characteristics tab

A quality inspection is conducted to confirm the acceptability of a product for its intended purpose. During the inspection process, the results for

inspection characteristics are recorded and compared with predefined quality requirements. On the basis of this comparison, individual characteristics are accepted or rejected. At the conclusion of the inspection, on the basis of inspection characteristic valuations, a usage decision is documented for the inspection lot. To identify the characteristics that are relevant to a usage decision, a user can display characteristic results that have been documented for one or more than one inspection lots. Characteristic results can be displayed in chronological order with the Results History function, which is accessed with the Usage Decision or Results Recording functions.

Q-195:   C. Record Usage Decision and D. Confirm Activities for Operations

A quality inspection is conducted to confirm the acceptability of a product for its intended purpose. During the inspection process, the results for inspection characteristics are recorded and compared with predefined quality requirements. On the basis of this comparison, individual characteristics are accepted or rejected. At the conclusion of the inspection, on the basis of inspection characteristic valuations, a usage decision is documented for the inspection lot. The Confirm Activities for Operations is another function of the Inspection Lot completion component.

Q-196:   A. Track the appraisal costs incurred at a work center for activities performed in an operation and B. Confirm times for activity types to a QM order when inspection results or usage decision is recorded

Quality Management orders are used to collect and manage quality costs that are incurred in the performance of QM activities. The orders are the means by which activities that support the processing of quality inspections are linked to cost assignment objects in the Controlling component. To capture appraisal costs that originate with a particular inspection lot, a QM order is created when the inspection lot is created, the order is assigned to a material and/or inspection lot. Next, quality costs, in the form of activity times, are assigned to activity types and subsequently confirmed to a QM order. Then, the confirmed activities are settled to the appropriate cost assignment object(s) in the Controlling component.

Q-197:   A. Material in inspection lot has been posted from inspection stock to unrestricted stock

A stock posting documents the entry or removal of a manufactured or procured material to or from stock. The stock posting ensures that the material in a stock-relevant inspection lot is properly accounted for, which contributes to effective logistics management and financial propriety. The Inspection Lot Completion component includes the functions necessary to make stock postings. For example, as a usage decision is recorded, the system can automatically propose a stock account to which the material in an inspection lot may be posted. The stock account is proposed according to control indicators that are set for usage decision codes, which are recorded at the conclusion of the quality inspection. In the event that a stock posting was made in error, it can be reversed. To do so requires the original entry of a usage decision for an inspection lot, a stock posting for the transfer of stock from inspection stock to unrestricted use stock, the creation of a return delivery with reference to the original purchase order and the cancellation of the inspection lot.

Q-198:   B. List of material documents for inspection lots

A stock posting documents the entry or removal of a manufactured or procured material to or from stock. The stock posting ensures that the material in a stock-relevant inspection lot is properly accounted for, which contributes to effective logistics management and financial propriety. The Inspection Lot Completion component includes the functionality necessary to display stock that has been posted to or from a particular inspection lot and to make additional stock postings. The list of material documents for inspection lots can be used to review the stock transfers between storage locations and the stock postings that occur simultaneously with usage decisions.

Q-199:   A. Display stock posted at the creation of inspection lot

A stock posting documents the entry or removal of a manufactured or procured material to or from stock. The stock posting ensures that the material in a stock-relevant inspection lot is properly accounted for, which contributes to effective logistics management and financial propriety. The Inspection Lot Completion component includes the functionality necessary to display stock that has been posted to or from a particular inspection lot and to make additional stock postings. The list of material documents for inspection lots can be used to review the stock transfers between storage locations and the stock postings that occur simultaneously with usage decisions.

Q-200:   A. Usage Decision - Overview of Stocks

A stock posting documents the entry or removal of a manufactured or procured material to or from stock. The stock posting ensures that the material in a stock-relevant inspection lot is properly accounted for, which contributes to effective logistics management and

financial propriety. The Inspection Lot Completion component includes the functionality necessary to make stock postings before, during or after a usage decision is recorded. You can also view the stock in the inspection lot and then post the inspected materials to the appropriate stock account. The Usage Decision – Overview of Stocks is used for this purpose.

Q-201:   B. Evaluations – QMIS

A quality inspection is conducted to confirm the acceptability of a product for its intended purpose. During the inspection process, the results for inspection characteristics are recorded and compared with predefined quality requirements. On the basis of this comparison, individual characteristics are accepted or rejected. At the conclusion of the inspection, on the basis of inspection characteristic valuations, a usage decision is documented for the inspection lot. The Evaluations – QMIS function is used to display inspection results for more than one inspection lot.